What people are saying about …

THE SPIRIT WHO SPEAKS

"There is no denying that the Holy Spirit speaks today, but we find it hard to hear Him and discern His leading. *The Spirit Who Speaks* revealed new truths to me, reminded me of truths I knew but had forgotten, and reinforced truths I treasure. This is an insightful and inspiring book."

J.John, speaker and author of over fifty books, including *TEN: Laws of Love Set in Stone*

"Written with humor, honesty, and good biblical grounding, this book tells the story of a man trying to hear and respond to God's Spirit talking to him."

Mark Melluish, regional director of New Wine London and Southeast

THE
SPIRIT
WHO
SPEAKS

THE
SPIRIT
WHO
SPEAKS

GOD'S SUPERNATURAL
INTERVENTION IN YOUR LIFE

PETER H. LAWRENCE

David C Cook®

transforming lives together

THE SPIRIT WHO SPEAKS
Published by David C Cook
4050 Lee Vance View
Colorado Springs, CO 80918 U.S.A.

David C Cook Distribution Canada
55 Woodslee Avenue, Paris, Ontario, Canada N3L 3E5

David C Cook U.K., Kingsway Communications
Eastbourne, East Sussex BN23 6NT, England

The website addresses recommended throughout this book are offered as a
resource to you. These websites are not intended in any way to be or imply an
endorsement on the part of David C Cook, nor do we vouch for their content.

Unless otherwise noted, all Scripture quotations are taken from the Holy
Bible, New International Version®, NIV®. Copyright © 1973, 1978, 1984 by
Biblica, Inc™. Used by permission of Zondervan. All rights reserved worldwide.
www.zondervan.com. Scripture quotations marked NKJV are taken from the
New King James Version. Copyright © 1982 by Thomas Nelson, Inc. Used by
permission. All rights reserved; RSV are taken from the Revised Standard Version
Bible, copyright 1952 [2nd edition, 1971], Division of Christian Education
of the National Council of the Churches of Christ in the United States of
America. Used by permission. All rights reserved; ESV are taken from *The Holy
Bible, English Standard Version.* Copyright © 2000; 2001 by Crossway Bibles, a
division of Good News Publishers. Used by permission. All rights reserved.
The author has added italics to Scripture quotations for emphasis.

LCCN 2011921846
ISBN 978-1-4347-6529-1
eISBN 978-1-4347-0370-5

© 2011 Peter H. Lawrence

The Team: Richard Herkes, Karen Lee-Thorp, Sarah
Schultz, Renada Arens, and Karen Athen
Cover Design: Amy Konyndyk

Printed in the United States of America
First Edition 2011

1 2 3 4 5 6 7 8 9 10

062911

CONTENTS

FOREWORD 9

PREFACE 13

1. THE GOD WHO SPEAKS 15

2. IS THERE A WORD FROM THE LORD? 35

3. THE ADVENTURE OF PRAYER 53

4. PROCLAIM THE KING AND THE KINGDOM 77

5. HEALING THE EMOTIONS 99

6. HEALING THE SICK 125

7. SETTING THE CAPTIVES FREE 145

8. SIGNS AND BLUNDERS 165

9. TEST EVERYTHING 185

10. FACING THE END 209

STUDY GUIDE 223

NOTES 237

FOREWORD

Every generation or two the pendulum swings with regard to the Spirit's work in the church. One generation is overly cautious and grieves the Spirit by marginalizing or ignoring Him. The next generation decides that is the wrong approach and goes full bore ahead with little to no discernment, only to grieve the Spirit by attributing to Him all manner of craziness. The next generation then reacts with caution. On and on that wheel rolls through the history of the church.

But there is a better way, a third way. I call this a "safe and sane" way to engage with the Spirit in ways that are *adult* and discerning, and simultaneously full of *childlike* faith and passionate pursuit. It seems to me that if one reads the stories of the Gospels and adds up all the pastoral advice contained in the New Testament letters, you come to something like this: Go! Move forward! Have faith! Be a child, not a cynical adult! *But* ... use your head. Use the Golden Rule as you go. Don't just get gifts and power—get character as you go. Don't just get *engifted*—get *enfruited!*

John Wimber, and the churches he founded, Vineyard Churches, while not perfect by any means, certainly do not need a defense by me. John and his work will stand well the test of time and the judgment of church history. But because Peter Lawrence was so impacted by John, and because so much of his story is attached to Vineyard ministries, it may be useful for readers of this book to understand a bit about Wimber and the values and practices he developed regarding the ministry in the Spirit.

The basic controlling idea for John was this: He wanted, for himself and for the churches he led, all of the Holy Spirit he could possibly receive this side of heaven. He wanted to be a pentecostal, with a lower case *p*. But he did not accept Pentecostal explanations of the reception of the Spirit. He was also leery of many practices of Pentecostals of the mid- to late twentieth century. He was trying to find a third way.

John, in my view as a close colleague, did in fact find a third way, a means of moving forward that was both faith-filled and sensible. He taught values I believe ought to mark engagement with the Spirit at all times and in all places:

Keep it real—do nothing for effect or to be seen by others.

Never manipulate people—love them and treat them as you would want to be treated.

Never hype stories—the Spirit is capable of handling His own PR.

Go for it—but as child, as a learner, as an apprentice, never acting the part of an expert.

Follow the Scriptures, let the Scripture set the *norms* for what it means to engage with the Spirit.

Finally, act with discernment, but not fear—knowing you are children of your Father in heaven who knows how to give good gifts—the Holy Spirit—to those He loves (Luke 11:9–13).

Christianity without a rich interactive relationship with God the Holy Spirit is subbiblical. Peter Lawrence guides readers to a safe and sane, yet powerful engagement with the Spirit—the Spirit who does indeed speak to those childlike souls who listen with a heart to hear and the will to humbly discern His voice.

Todd Hunter
Anglican Bishop
Former President, Vineyard Churches, USA
Author of *Christianity Beyond Belief, Giving Church Another Chance,*
The Outsider Interviews, and *The Accidental Anglican*

PREFACE

My husband, Peter, was a vicar in the Church of England for thirty-two years. For the last fourteen years he led the three churches of Canford Magna in Dorset. He was interested in things of the Spirit from the time of his training for the ministry and longed to see God at work in people's lives. As well as leading churches, he accepted invitations to speak on life in the Spirit in many places all over the country and sometimes overseas.

One aspect of life in the Spirit essential to Peter was hearing the Spirit speak. Is there such a thing as a "word" from the Lord today? Can anyone hear God speak? How do we know it is God who is speaking? This book answers these questions. Not all "words" that people claim are from God are helpful. Many of us have heard someone well meaning say they have a word from God, which ends up causing harm—not the advancement of God's kingdom. That is why testing a word and the way it is given is so important. Peter writes with clarity and insight—and from much experience—about these issues in chapter nine.

Several people have asked me how someone who wrote and preached about hearing God speak and saw God healing others could himself suffer from a terminal illness. My response is that they need to listen more carefully to what Peter is saying. He writes about his illness and talks about questions such as this in the final chapter of this book.

Peter died in February 2009 from a brain tumor. He had been ill for about a year and a half, and during that time he wrote *The Spirit Who Speaks* based on one of his earlier books (*The Hot Line*). He was thrilled to sign the contract for publication of this book—which he could just about manage to do—in January of that year.

Peter had a great gift for teaching the Bible and theology in a way that all could understand. He was also very down-to-earth and wise concerning how to put into practice the things of the Spirit. Not many are good at both the theory and the practice. Peter writes as he taught, in a relaxed but profound way.

Carol Lawrence
October 2010

1

THE GOD WHO SPEAKS

The speaker at our conference looked like Santa Claus. He had a big belly, a full beard, a jovial smile, and an American accent. There were several thousand of us in the Sheffield Centre in Britain in 1985 who had been persuaded against our better judgment to attend a conference with the not-at-all-British title "Signs and Wonders."

Santa played a keyboard to the highest standard and led us in a time of musical worship. (I discovered afterward that he arranged songs for the Righteous Brothers and actually had three top-ten hits in America, all at the same time.) He then came to the lectern, told the story of how he had become a Christian, and regaled us with all kinds of stories and jokes for an hour. I was captivated and enjoyed myself immensely.

In the evening there was much more teaching from the Bible, emphasizing Jesus' dependence on His Father. Jesus said, "I tell you the truth, the Son can do nothing by himself; he can do only what he sees his Father doing, because whatever the Father does the Son also does" (John 5:19).

Our speaker placed the emphasis on Jesus, full of the Holy Spirit, taking His orders from His Father. Jesus teaches us what the Father teaches Him (John 7:17), He speaks what the Father speaks (John 8:2–11), and He says what the Father says (John 14:10). All of which comes from the Father through the Spirit: "For the one whom God has sent speaks the words of God, for God gives the Spirit without limit" (John 3:34).

And then the speaker, whose name was John Wimber, had a go at speaking a "word."

"Is there a lady here," he asked, "aged thirty-two, with a bad throat, with a name beginning with *L*, who would be willing to come out?"

I had never witnessed anything like this before, so it was good we had heard John's testimony and his teaching from the Bible beforehand. It could have been a put-up job, but I trusted him. When the "word" was given, Linda sensed the Spirit speak to her, and she came down from the back quite quickly.

During the interview it was obvious she had a bad throat, but she was adamant that her age was thirty-one, not thirty-two. A team prayed for her; she went down on the floor, and when she came up, her voice was clear and seemed to be healed. It was impressive. But there was no way I could have possibly guessed what Santa's sack had for me next.

"Is there someone here," John asked, "whose testicle did not drop as a teenager?" What a question! What an embarrassment! It was me. Fortunately the stage was full of people receiving prayer for other "words," so John said it might be better if the person saw him privately afterward. Good job!

Just before the conference a surgeon had seen me and advised that I have my testicle removed in case it turned cancerous. He booked me in for an operation when I returned from Yorkshire. After the service, I checked to see if anyone else had claimed the word—apparently not.

Sadly, nobody could find John Wimber to pray for me, so I saw a curate, and the next day a bishop. I wasn't healed and I had the operation, but I had much to think about. It appears not only that God *can* still speak to us today, but He is willing to do so.

First Attempts

I came home from Sheffield on Wednesday and had one day to prepare for a celebration meeting in our church, at which our bishop was preaching. Should I or shouldn't I—have a go, that is? I decided if God gave me a word, I would give it. During the meeting I got a twinge in my left thumb and thought it might be from God. The speakers at Sheffield had told us that pain in our bodies can sometimes be a word from the Spirit of God for somebody He wants to heal, so I tried it.

"Is there anyone here who has something wrong with their left thumb?" I asked hopefully, after the bishop had spoken.

Now you would have thought that in a group of 150 people there would be somebody with something wrong with a left thumb, but apparently not. The bishop looked at me—should he close with the blessing? I nodded, and he dismissed the crowd.

As people began filing out, a young man made his way forward to see me. "I cut my left thumb opening a tin," he said apologetically, "but I didn't like to mention it in front of all those people."

Go away, I thought, *it's no good now.* Inwardly I was screaming, *Come back, everyone, the thumb's here!* But it was too late. I thanked him for coming forward, prayed for him, and then crawled home, mumbling as I went.

Greg, a man from our church, rang to encourage me the next day, which was totally unexpected and very welcome, as I thought I might need to start looking for a new job. Thus reaffirmed, and having thought things through a little, I tried again, this time with our young people on Sunday night.

Roger Jones, our director of music, had come to talk to the youth, and after he'd finished, we waited upon God. Immediately thoughts flashed into my mind: *Toe, back, eye.* This was crazy stuff. It was a young people's meeting and there were only nine or ten present. If I'd received such words at our over-sixties group, I'd have felt more confident. At this point Roger began to cough painfully, and I knew he often suffered from a sore throat, so I said to God, "What about this man, Lord?" The answer came back, "Not on the agenda." So I gave it a try: "Anyone here with a pain in the toe, back, or eye?" I asked, feeling very unsure of myself. Three teenage lads claimed one each and we divided up to pray for them.

The one with the pain in the back said he'd only begun to feel pain when he sat on the chair in the room. We were very slow to realize that these three were our most skeptical members; two of them claimed to be unbelievers. With hindsight and more experience, I now believe the Holy Spirit gave those three words about very small complaints to show three people, who in varying degrees were struggling with unbelief, how much He loved them. Clearly, if I'd had a word about "two unbelievers and a skeptic," everyone would have said I knew that anyway. No one knew of the physical complaints mentioned, especially as one had only cropped up at the time. Had we not been so dim-witted, we might have used the Spirit's words more lovingly and profitably.

Nevertheless, I was encouraged. We carried on with the ministry on Sunday evenings and in our small midweek meetings, and learned not to despise "the day of small things" (Zech. 4:10). I enthused about the conference and shared with my friends whenever the Spirit came and did something significant among us. Occasionally people received a picture or a sense of peace, but most commonly we received "word[s] of knowledge" (1 Cor. 12:8 NKJV).

I shared a few of these things with an acquaintance from another church and then half-jokingly said, "Get me an invitation to one of your services and I'll come and do a Wimber on your congregation." This was a very silly thing to say. She took me seriously and a letter arrived from her vicar inviting me to speak and minister at a Thursday night celebration in January. I was too embarrassed to refuse.

I meditated upon the problem and then ransacked my library in search of confidence-boosting fodder. I was looking for something on words from God. I needed some quotations to add authenticity to my message, and eventually my eyes rested on a book by Stuart Blanch, a former archbishop of York. Like several of the books in my study, it was unread, but I thought a casual aside from an archbishop would sound impressive. I read the first eleven pages, usually enough to find a decent quote, but then found myself putting the book down in total amazement. One sentence stopped me in my tracks: "The Bible … rests on the assumption that God speaks."[1] With all the "words of knowledge" we had been getting, this spoke volumes to me.

It was what my friend Bishop John Finney would describe as a "blob" experience—a moment of insight, a sudden encounter with truth. In the past few months I had been thrilled to hear the Spirit speaking to me and had paraded my stories in the pulpit like a centenarian with a telegram from the Queen. Most of us think God may, from time to time, beam in with a special word on special occasions for special people. I had likewise exhibited my words from the Holy Spirit as trophies or rewards for good conduct, as evidence of my high spiritual standing, but suddenly that lie was exposed. God is a God who speaks! Just as I am a man who eats, God is a God who speaks. On Sundays nobody asks me if I've eaten anything in the past week; everyone assumes I have. I am a man who eats; it is part of my very nature as a man and something I do without thinking. God is a God who speaks; the Bible declares it from beginning to end.

As the penny dropped, I recognized in myself a wrong-thinking about God. People are inconsistent. Even the mature saint fails to do good all the time. We cannot always discern accurately who a person is from what a person does. If a Christian preacher confesses to spending a night with a prostitute, as some have done, we cannot easily tell if it is the confession of a "con man" who has been found out or a sinner who is repentant. There are two kingdoms at war within us, and at different moments either might be seen to have the upper hand.

But God is not like that. His nature is perfect, incorruptible, and totally consistent. He always reveals His true character in everything He does. We may not interpret all He does correctly, because we see through a glass darkly due to our sinful natures, but when so many believers over so many centuries have encountered the God who speaks by His Spirit, it seems right to conclude this is part of who He is. The Bible rests on the assumption that God is a God who speaks.

My whole being thrilled to this new concept, but with the excitement came a twinge of fear. *If this is true,* I thought, *then I can expect the Spirit of God to speak to me regularly. And if I preach it as true, the congregation will expect the Spirit to speak to them.* This was a moment of truth for me! I began to realize why some of my ancestors had denied the present-day existence of spiritual gifts and settled for a more comfortable way of life. It is always much easier to claim that God *has* spoken and God *will* speak than that God *speaks*. All my past hurts, fears, rejections, and psychological hang-ups surfaced at once, as my yearning for security sought to bury this simple, luminous truth in the ground, like the man in the Bible did with his one talent (Matt. 25:14–30). As a vicar, I had always sought to hide my insecure emotions by commenting on life rather than risk taking part in it, and yet I couldn't bear the thought of spending the rest of my days running away from truth in search of a quiet life.

I decided to think through this new concept and prepare my sermon for the evening service at my friend's church accordingly. If, after investigating, I still thought God is a God who speaks, I would expect Him to validate His word. I asked myself three important questions:

1. Does the Bible rest on the assumption that God speaks?

2. Does God speak by His Holy Spirit today?

3. In what way does the Holy Spirit speak today?

Does the Bible Assume God Speaks?

The Bible opens with these words: "In the beginning God created." The way He created was by speaking: "God *said*, 'Let there be light,' and there was light" (Gen. 1:3). As the psalmist says, "The heavens declare the glory of God" (Ps. 19:1).

As soon as mankind appears, God speaks to them. He speaks to Adam and Eve and to their family; He speaks to Noah, Abraham, and the patriarchs. From Moses to Malachi, the prophets thunder, "Thus says the Lord."

He speaks to the world through Jesus, the Word of God. The writer to the Hebrews says, "In many and various ways God spoke of old to our fathers by the prophets; but in these last days he has spoken to us by a Son" (Heb. 1:1–2 RSV). On the day of Pentecost the Spirit of God was poured out for all believers: "The promise is for you and your children and for all who are far off—for all whom the Lord our God will call" (Acts 2:39), and it is through the Spirit's gift of tongues (languages)—God speaking—that the world is alerted to this truth.

Paul assures us that God, the God who loves to speak, is now dwelling in every believer by His Spirit. "If anyone does not have the Spirit of Christ, he does not belong to Christ" (Rom. 8:9). "We were all baptized by one Spirit" (1 Cor. 12:13); "You are the body of Christ" (1 Cor. 12:27). The gifts of the Spirit that Paul talks about are nearly all gifts that enable us to hear God speaking or discern what He is doing. And the final book of the Bible continues on the same theme: "He who has an ear, let him hear what the Spirit says to the churches" (Rev. 2:7).

This revelation about God is present from beginning to end of the Bible—and it is present as a powerful truth. If we compare the statement "God speaks" with other biblical statements like "God heals" or "God loves" or "God forgives," we can appreciate its strength. Anyone who says "God heals" has to have something to say about the plagues He sent upon Egypt (Ex. 9:8–11; 12:29), the leprosy He gave to Gehazi (2 Kings 5:27), and the blindness He gave to Elymas (Acts 13:9–12). Even in Revelation, John tells us that at the end of history God will not heal everyone (Rev. 20:11–15).

Anyone who says "God forgives" has to have something to say about "God judges," and those who claim "God loves sinners" can never forget that "God hates sin." It is far easier to claim that God "speaks" than that God heals, forgives, or loves. Whether He is saving Daniel (Dan. 6:22), killing Ananias and Sapphira (Acts 5:5, 10), forgiving a woman caught in the act of adultery (John 8:11b), urging the stoning of a man to death for collecting sticks on the Sabbath (Num. 15:32–36), whipping the money-changers with cords (John 2:15), or accepting lashes Himself (Mark 15:15), God is speaking. Even when He is silent, He communicates: "Again the Israelites did evil in the eyes of the LORD, and for seven years he gave them into the hands of the Midianites" (Judg. 6:1). Verses 7 and 8 continue, "When the Israelites cried to the LORD because of Midian, he sent them a prophet."

There are times in Scripture and in the history of the church when the word of the Lord has been rare (e.g., 1 Sam. 3:1), but it seems to have been the result of people's sin rather than God's unwillingness to speak (1 Sam. 2:12–36). In Genesis 1—2, Adam and Eve had fellowship with God, but after they sinned in chapter 3, they hid from Him. It appears that sin causes us to turn our backs on God, while the saving activity of God enables us to turn around, face Him, and call Him Father. God has recalled us into fellowship through His Son, Jesus Christ (1 Cor. 1:9); Paul prays for the "fellowship of the Holy Spirit" to be with the Corinthians (2 Cor. 13:14); and John says, "Our fellowship is with the Father and with his Son, Jesus Christ" (1 John 1:3). God's desire is to have fellowship with His children, and salvation through Jesus restores us into that fellowship. A God who creates us for fellowship—and calls us back into fellowship through repentance and faith—is a God who loves to communicate with His children.

Jeremiah 10:10 says, "But the LORD is the true God; he is the living God," and Paul teaches about God's spiritual gifts that enable us to discern His activity and hear His voice.

The God of Isaiah (Isa. 37:17), Jeremiah (Jer. 23:36), Daniel (Dan. 6:26), Hosea (Hos. 1:10), Jesus (John 6:57), Peter (Matt. 16:16), Paul (Acts 14:15), the writer to the Hebrews (Heb. 12:22), and John (Rev. 7:2) is a "living God." He is not a dumb idol but a God who speaks.

If we accept the biblical revelation, it seems we are on firm ground when we claim that the living God, who lives in all believers by His Holy Spirit, is a God who speaks.

Does God Speak Today?

In a world of changing pressures and insecurities, the Bible has always been very precious to me. Ever since my conversion at fourteen, the foundation of my Christian faith has been the Scriptures, and I firmly believe the Spirit speaks to us today through them. Every day I try to spend time reading from the Bible, asking the Holy Spirit to speak to me through God's Word.

Most Christians accept that God communicates through the Bible, but some go on to say that today God speaks to us *only* through the Bible. It is this "only" that concerns me. I was brought up to believe in a God who has spoken and will one day speak again, but for the present speaks only through His written Word—lest we should be tossed about by every whim and fancy. I believe the main way God speaks to us today is through the Bible, but I do not believe it is the only way God speaks. I spent some time thinking about this and found three reasons why I could no longer accept that the Spirit speaks today *only* through Scripture.

Logic

We present an enormous credibility gap to our secular age if we preach a different God from the one found in the Bible. It is very difficult to convince the world of a God who spoke directly to Moses and Elijah and Peter and Paul, but will not speak directly to us today. If people learn of a God who is the same yesterday, today, and forever, who speaks directly to people for several thousand years, but then stops because He's got a book out, it is not surprising if they turn away. The unbeliever is often very quick to see through logical inconsistency. If a book cannot be validated by experience, it is normally classified as "fiction." If the Bible rests on the assumption that God speaks, it seems logical to believe He still speaks today, unless the Bible has told us otherwise.

Experience

Historical and contemporary experiences support the view that God did not stop speaking upon the completion of the New Testament. George Fox, founder of the Quakers; Evan Roberts, whom God used in the Welsh Revival of 1904; Smith Wigglesworth, who brought Pentecostal revival to many; and David Yonggi Cho, pastor of the world's largest church, in Korea, are just four of the many people who have claimed the Spirit of God spoke to them with signs following. The faith of all of these men was rooted in the Bible; Smith Wigglesworth would read no other book. All four were Bible-based believers, teachers, and preachers, but none were "Bible-only" advocates. Their experiences validated the Bible, and the Bible validated their experiences. They all encountered the Spirit who speaks in the Bible and in their own Christian lives.

The Bible

Biblical Christianity is about being sons and daughters of the King, being the bride of Christ, having communion with God, knowing God, and being known by Him. Through the Spirit we may know God (Heb. 8:11), know His voice (John 10:4), know the truth (John 16:13), and know the mind of Christ (1 Cor. 2:16). I was unable to find anything in the New Testament to suggest the promises God made to the disciples and the early church are not meant for us as well. After the Spirit speaks on the day of Pentecost, Peter promises that the gift of the Holy Spirit is "for all" (Acts 2:39). When we see God face-to-face, then the spiritual gifts will cease, but the New Testament gives no indication of this occurring before then (1 Cor. 13:9–10).

The canon of Scripture is closed. This means the promises and teachings of the New Testament must apply to us today, otherwise we would need a third set of canonical writings to explain the new rules. The people in the Old Testament lived under the old covenant. The people of the New Testament lived under the new covenant. As there has not been a third covenant between God and His people, it is right to assume we also live under the new covenant sealed by the blood of Jesus Christ. This must surely mean the promises and teachings of the new covenant apply to all Christians today.

To say the New Testament teachings no longer apply to us is to add a new interpretation of Scripture, invariably based on experience—or lack of it—rather than what the Bible teaches. "I have not heard the Spirit speak," so God does not speak. "I have not healed the sick," so God no longer heals the sick. "I do not speak in tongues," so the gift has died out. At the conference in Sheffield, John Wimber exposed the woolliness of this thinking when he said, "We do not seek to bring Scripture down to our experience, but rather we seek to bring our experience up to Scripture."

This is what the Bible encourages us to do. It teaches us that anyone who has faith in Jesus will do what He did (John 14:12); the Holy Spirit is promised to "everyone who calls on the name of the Lord … for you and your children and for all who are far off" (Acts 2:21, 39); all under the new covenant will know God "from the least of them to the greatest" (Heb. 8:11) and receive His words in their mouths:

> "As for me, this is my covenant with them," says the
> LORD. "My Spirit, who is on you, and my words
> that I have put in your mouth will not depart from

your mouth, or from the mouths of your children,
or from the mouths of their descendants from this
time on and forever," says the LORD. (Isa. 59:21)

I believe in the Bible. I believe God speaks to us today through the
Scriptures. I believe God also speaks to us today by His Holy Spirit.

In What Way Does the Spirit Speak Today?

After deciding I believe in a God who speaks today, I began to feel the
ground shaking a little beneath my feet. If God speaks today by His
Spirit, does this undermine the authority of Scripture? What is the
relationship between the written Word of God and the living word
of God? Does a word from the Lord today equal the importance of
the Bible? I recognized some of the dangers immediately.

In the last book of the Bible we read these words:

I warn everyone who hears the words of the
prophecy of this book: If anyone adds anything to
them, God will add to him the plagues described
in this book. And if anyone takes words away from
this book of prophecy, God will take away from
him his share in the tree of life and in the holy city,
which are described in this book. (Rev. 22:18–19)

We should be very cautious about anyone who claims to have
subsequent revelations from the Holy Spirit that either add to or
take away from Scripture. Muhammad and Joseph Smith claimed
subsequent revelations from God that produced the Qur'an and

the Book of Mormon, respectively, and the list of today's self-styled cultic prophets who seek to lead people away from God's truth is endless.

Heeding the New Testament's warning against adding to or taking away from its message, I turned to that message again in an attempt to understand the relationship between the Word of God and a word from God.

> The holy Scriptures … are able to make you wise for salvation through faith in Christ Jesus. All Scripture is God-breathed and is useful for teaching, rebuking, correcting and training in righteousness, so that the man of God may be thoroughly equipped for every good work. (2 Tim. 3:15–17)

One of the reasons the Holy Spirit inspired the writing of Scripture was for the purposes of doctrine and teaching, especially the way of salvation through faith in Jesus. This is the Word of God. It is God-breathed and therefore carries the authority of God Himself (cf. 2 Peter 1:20–21; 1 Cor. 2:13). But there is another reason for treating the Bible as authoritative:

> We did not follow cleverly invented stories when we told you about the power and coming of our Lord Jesus Christ, but we were eyewitnesses of his majesty.… We ourselves heard this voice that came from heaven when we were with him on the sacred mountain. (2 Peter 1:16, 18)

> That which was from the beginning, which we have
> heard, which we have seen with our eyes, which we
> have looked at and our hands have touched—this we
> proclaim concerning the Word of life. (1 John 1:1)

The second letter of Peter and the first letter of John appeared at a time when false teachers and prophets were becoming active (2 Peter 2; 1 John 4:1). It was no longer sufficient for the disciples to say their writings had the authority of the Holy Spirit, because many other heretical teachers were claiming the same thing. The unique authority of the New Testament writers came from the inspiration of the Holy Spirit and their credibility as eyewitnesses to the earthly Jesus. They could match up the words of the Spirit with those of the earthly Lord Jesus whom they had known and loved. Until the second coming of Jesus, this authority will remain unique.

The canon of Scripture is closed because it carries the unique authority of Jesus Himself. The Old Testament anticipates and prepares for His coming, the Gospels describe His coming, and the Epistles testify to the effect of His coming. The Gospels and Epistles have authority because they came from those in touch with the early disciples who knew the earthly Jesus.

In Acts 1, Peter outlines the necessary requirements for election as an apostle:

> It is necessary to choose one of the men who have
> been with us the whole time the Lord Jesus went in
> and out among us, beginning from John's baptism
> to the time when Jesus was taken up from us. For

one of these must become a witness with us of his
resurrection. (Acts 1:21–22)

An apostle therefore had to be an eyewitness of the life and
resurrection of the Lord Jesus Christ. They were the special people
whose role was to teach (Acts 2:42; 4:2) and to be guardians of the
faith (e.g., Acts 15:2). There are obviously no such eyewitnesses alive
today, and the canon of Scripture is closed.

Paul's writings were accepted into the New Testament because
others who knew Jesus gave them authority. Although we believe
that Paul did not know the earthly Jesus, Peter authenticates Paul's
letters as Scripture.

Our dear brother Paul also wrote you with the
wisdom that God gave him. He writes the same
way in all his letters, speaking in them of these
matters. His letters contain some things that are
hard to understand, which ignorant and unstable
people distort, as they do the other Scriptures.
(2 Peter 3:15–16)

If for no other reason, then, Paul's letters stand as the Word of
God because those who knew the earthly Jesus, such as Peter, validated them. He described them as "Scriptures."

This means the Word of God has the authority of the earthly
Jesus, plus that of the Holy Spirit who inspired their writing. The
same Holy Spirit is present among us today, as He was in the early
church, but the earthly Jesus and witnesses of His earthly life are no

longer present to check things out. Jesus is here by His Spirit, but not in the flesh; we cannot see Him face-to-face, so we cannot test words from God except by Scripture. Thus a word from God today must not contain any new teaching; neither must it add to or take away from the doctrines of the Bible. It seems right to say that a present-day word from God may therefore illustrate Scripture, help to apply Scripture, authenticate Scripture, and enable Christians to fulfill the commands of Scripture, but must always be tested by Scripture. This enables us to understand the different purposes behind the Word of God and a word from God.

In Romans 10:9, Paul writes, "If you confess with your mouth, 'Jesus is Lord,' and believe in your heart that God raised him from the dead, you will be saved." This is doctrine and teaches us the way of salvation. Such teaching is one of the main purposes of the Word of God.

In Acts 8:29, we read, "The Spirit told Philip, 'Go to that chariot and stay near it.'" Although it is part of the Word of God and teaches us the value of letting the Holy Spirit direct evangelism, this also provides an illustration of a word from God. It is a piece of local and particular guidance given to Philip by the Holy Spirit for one man in one place at one time. It is a word *from* God that enables Philip to fulfill the Word *of* God, going to that chariot, witnessing to that Ethiopian, and leading him to faith in Christ.

Through the Bible God speaks about the way to be saved and to live as Christians, and through His Spirit, God applies that truth to the right person in the right place at the right time. We could say a word from God released by the Holy Spirit supports the Word of God inspired by the Holy Spirit, helping Christians to live out its principles.

The example of a word from the Spirit that I witnessed in Sheffield illustrates this. The Bible tells us to proclaim the kingdom, heal the sick, and cast out demons. The Spirit's word about Linda helped John Wimber do those very things, in the name of Jesus, on the first night of the conference. The Bible gives doctrinal truth and general guidelines, whereas God sends a specific word by His Holy Spirit to give particular guidance. We should therefore keep, study, and regularly teach from the Bible, but discard words from God once we've acted upon their messages. The Bible teaches us doctrine and basic truths, and the Spirit speaks today to help us put those biblical truths into practice. Anything that contradicts Scripture or takes away from it is to be rejected at once as not of God, but a current word or nudge from God by His Spirit can help us apply the teaching of the Bible to our daily lives. A word from God can be expected to support the Word of God.

My thinking and sermon preparations were now complete. Biblically, logically, theologically, and, in a limited way, experientially, I knew God to be a God who speaks. I knew that God wanted me to proclaim this truth when I went to my friend's church in January.

2

IS THERE A WORD FROM THE LORD?

A Christmas Eve Debut

I came home from the hospital in November 1985, the offending article removed, and my thoughts turned to Christmas. Small signs and baby wonders were beginning to pop up from time to time, and I was encouraged to take slightly larger steps of faith as I believed the Holy Spirit directed me.

"When is it really going to happen, Lord?" I inquired. I paused and waited for an answer. "Christmas Eve," I thought God said, "at the midnight communion service."

Now that was a thought pregnant with possibilities: *full church—some real outsiders present—everyone relaxed and happy through inebriation.* Our church was not far from a local drinking establishment, and it was amazing to see who used to find their way into our Christmas Eve service after "chucking out" time. It was an amusing thought, but also a serious one. "You will receive power when the Holy Spirit comes on you," said Jesus, "and you will be my witnesses" (Acts 1:8). The coming of God's Spirit often accomplishes many things, but evangelism has top billing in Acts. I began to take the idea on board, wondering if ministry in the Spirit would be more powerful and more welcomed among outsiders than Christians.

"What shall I do, Lord?" I asked. More impressions in my mind: "Invite twenty people on whom you have seen the Spirit come to meet with you on Christmas Eve at 10:00 p.m. They will be your ministry team. Pray together first and then ask Me to speak to them in the service."

As I racked my brains to think of anyone on whom the Holy Spirit had made the slightest impact, from sixteen- to seventy-four-year-olds, I came up with eighteen names. My wife's parents, Gavin and Anne, were coming down for Christmas so that completed the twenty who duly received written invitations.

Nearer the time panic began to set in, followed by rigor mortis. "Help, Lord!" I pleaded. "How do I know it's You speaking?"

"What if I were to heal Mary's ears?" offered the other end of the dialogue. Mary suffered from very poor hearing, and I had been praying every day for her to be healed, ever since she had failed to claim a word for healing given at a meeting because she didn't hear it! "If you heal Mary's ears, Lord," I said, "I'll do anything you say." The discussion then continued on reasonably amicable lines. In my own mind this is what was agreed: At ten o'clock I would ask the Spirit to come on the gang of twenty, during which time I would speak healing in Jesus' name to Mary's ears. If they were healed I'd ask God to send His Spirit on the whole congregation later, and if not I'd do an ordinary service. This seemed a reasonable bargain and as I relaxed, life flowed back into my weary bones.

On Christmas Eve, I spent the whole day at the home of the Nursing Sisters of St. John the Divine, fasting, praying, sleeping (unscheduled), and reading the Bible. I felt I needed to throw everything into it and this was my way of taking God as seriously as I could.

While I was praying, the Holy Spirit led me to the Exodus story, and I read it through with excitement and encouragement. God called Moses, gave him a new ministry of signs and wonders, and sent him back to his people. Just like me. When Moses shared his new message with the Hebrew slaves, God showed them some signs and wonders that helped them to believe and support Moses in his new mission. Just like me. Moses went to Pharaoh with the promise of God and the backing of his people, and amazing things happened. God said, "'Take your staff and throw it down before Pharaoh,' and it will become a snake"—and it did (Ex. 7:9–10). God said, "Stretch out your staff and … the dust will become gnats"—and it did (Ex. 8:16–17). God said, "Stretch out your hand toward the sky so that darkness will spread over Egypt"—and it did (Ex. 10:21–22).

That's the way to do signs and wonders, I thought. I was sure I had the principle right. Through a series of miracles God set the Hebrews free, and many people believed. God said, "Lay hands on Mary's ears and they will be healed."

"May it be so, Lord," I prayed, "tonight." Just like Moses.

Encouraged and rested, though rather hungry, I met with most of the twenty at ten o'clock in the side-chapel of the church. I asked the Spirit to come and do what He wanted, and at an appropriate moment I laid hands on Mary's ears. "How do you feel, Mary?" I asked when I'd finished.

"Fine," she said, "very relaxed and blessed."

"How about the ears?" I inquired nonchalantly, not, of course, having dared share my "bargain" with anyone else.

"About the same," she said.

Suddenly others started sharing. "I saw a picture of a curtain," offered one, "and someone was pulling the wrong cord."

"Oh!" I said.

"I feel the Lord is saying you should preach evangelistically," chipped in a second.

"Yes," said a third, "with an appeal to come forward."

"Oh!" I said.

"I've got a real burden for the unsaved," volunteered a fourth. "We must tell them about Jesus and give them a chance to respond."

"Oh!" I said.

By now there were only a few minutes left before the service was due to start and I needed to robe. "Leave it with me," I concluded, and began to move. As I did so, Stephen, aged sixteen, stopped me and said, "It's not going to be easy, you know."

You can say that again, I thought. I'd never really made an appeal before and I didn't have an evangelistic sermon prepared.

I did my best. I wasn't very good. As I came to the challenge, I asked the ministry team to stand in the side aisles so the people could go to them if they wanted to receive Jesus. I thought this would make it easier for people to respond, but it turned out to be a big mistake. As believers surrounded the visitors on all sides, worry and pain registered on the faces of the imprisoned strangers; it looked a bit like the walls of Jericho, with the hosts of saints encamped around. When I asked people to go to the counselors if they wanted to accept Jesus, not a muscle twitched in the fearful, deep-frozen bodies I saw before me. I harangued them—encouraged them—tried to persuade them with every inch of my powerful personality, but not a soul moved. As verbal diarrhea began to set in, Christine, who was standing at the back, prayed, "Lord, please shut him up."

Unbelievably, I stopped in my tracks and uttered not another word. I wonder how many lay people down the centuries would have loved to receive the spiritual gift of shutting up their clergy that Christine exercised that night! We then waited in silence with no response.

As quickly as I could, I announced "Silent Night" as the next carol, which seemed appropriate at the time, and Jericho relaxed.

I cannot find words to express what I felt during the rest of the service. I suspect "white-hot anger" would be nearest the mark. My wife, Carol, commented afterward how the bread I gave her at the communion seemed to burn her. "Why, Lord?" I asked before I began the Eucharistic Prayer.

"Because I love you," He said, "like no one else."

I knew what He meant. No earthly father would have let me make such a fool of myself. I don't know how I managed the services the following morning, but I certainly didn't speak to God for several days after they were all over. The turkey had a different taste that year, and it felt like the worst Christmas Day of my life.

When I did eventually offer a prayer, the conversation in my mind went something like this: "OK, God. Tell me about it," I began.

"Read the Exodus story again," He said, "properly this time." So I did.

When Moses went to Pharaoh the first time, he had no opportunity to do any signs and wonders. Pharaoh not only sent Moses and Aaron packing, but he ordered the Hebrew slaves to make bricks without straw as a punishment (Ex. 5:7). I'd rather glossed over this bit on Christmas Eve.

The Israelite foremen went to Moses and Aaron when they returned and blamed them for the increased oppression, rather understandably. "Moses returned to the LORD and said, 'O Lord, why?'" (Ex. 5:22). The only answers I could find were in Exodus 6:2, "God … said to Moses, 'I am the LORD,'" and Exodus 6:6, "Say to the Israelites: 'I am the LORD.'" He ordered Moses to go back to Pharaoh.

"Will you still do everything I tell you to do?" God asked me. Pause. I took time to answer. Eventually I said, "There is no other. No other way, no other hope. I will continue to do whatever I think You are telling me to do. You are the Lord."

The Risk of Obedience

As I was going to sleep that night, an awful thought crept into my head about a young couple who attended our church. "Go and tell George and Alice that if they don't stop sleeping together, they'll never find me." I ignored it of course and went to sleep, but it was waiting for me when I awoke. I tried to shake it off all day, busying myself with good works, but the thought remained and nothing I could say or do would make it leave. Eventually I went to see George and Alice on a Tuesday night and stayed until midnight, but didn't even discover if they were going out with each other.

Twenty-four hours later, Wednesday night, there were fourteen at our midweek fellowship when I asked the Holy Spirit to come among us. People began prophesying and sharing pictures, and I was beginning to relax when more of those thoughts attacked me.

"There's somebody here with pain at the base of the spine; one with pain in the right knee; trouble with a nose, a tooth, and an ear."

I wasn't really in the mood for such intrusions, as the meeting was going well. I was well acquainted with every single person present, and since I knew no one who had any of these problems, I ignored the original thought and was just beginning to relax when an even nastier thought clobbered me. "You've disobeyed me once this week already. How many more times?" I'd promised to obey God whatever He said or did and I knew this was a turning point. With sheer embarrassment I tried to carry it off with a laugh: "I don't suppose there's anybody here with a pain in the back, right knee, or trouble with a nose, tooth, or ear?" Slowly all the words were claimed—one each.

Brian had damaged the base of his spine two days before, and I could have kicked myself for just saying "pain in the back." John was in such trouble with his right knee that he was contemplating giving up work. Greg had suffered with a blocked nose for many years; Jennifer was booked in at the dentist for a troublesome milk tooth. Angela's right ear had only started burning when I asked the Spirit to come—like the pain in the back that one of our unbelievers experienced after he came into the room on the earlier occasion. It seems God's Spirit sometimes gives physical symptoms in order to pinpoint a person to whom He wishes to minister, and it is an encouragement to all that God is present and active. We ministered to everyone that night, discovering various nonphysical problems as well, affirming one another and God's love for all of us. There were no dramatic physical healings, but John did not have to give up work.

The biggest encouragement—or concern—was that I seemed to have heard the Holy Spirit speaking. Although the words were not specifically detailed, five out of five in a group of fourteen was reasonable confirmation. This meant the other words were likely to be from God as well: "You've disobeyed me once this week already." It had to be referring to George and Alice, and I knew it. I was trapped by words that confirmed another word, and so eventually, two days before visiting my friend's church, I went for it.

"Forgive me if I'm wrong, but … I believe God may be saying … if you don't stop sleeping together, you'll never find Him."

George looked at the floor. Alice said, "What do you mean?"

Well, I thought I knew what I meant, but could only mutter, "I've just given the words as I've received them"—an important lesson, this one.

"The truth is," explained Alice, "we've been sleeping in the same bed together but never had sex."

Alice has now found God, but George never came to church again.

Struggling with God and wrestling with myself prepared me, without my realizing it, for what was to come next. I felt no great thrill in being right, as it was hardly a "successful" evening, but afterward I found that a quiet confidence in the Spirit had begun to grow within me, and a little more faith than before was now present. There are times when we experience the true depths of God's graciousness.

What Hearing the Spirit Feels Like

At a quarter to two on the same day as the meeting at my friend's church, I parked my car outside the crematorium chapel prior to doing a two o'clock funeral and switched the engine off. As I sat for a moment to compose myself, a wave of heat came across my forehead, so I closed my eyes and prayed, "Come, Holy Spirit." Physical sensations of greater heat and power came upon me, accompanied by a "knowing" in my mind that He was going to give me words for physical healing. Immediately I imagined a human body and, working my way upward in my mind, thought of a big toe, bowels, chest, mouth, and head.

When I tell people what it's like hearing the Spirit speak, they are usually disappointed when I cannot testify to blinding flashes, writing on the wall, or audible voices. Some people experience warmth, tingling, fluttering eyelids, a change in breathing rhythm, shaking, falling, and so on, all of which can be some of the physical phenomena that occur when the power of the Holy Spirit comes upon us. Such phenomena are not of themselves important—there is no advantage in lying on the floor as opposed to standing or sitting—but such things can be useful indications that God is present in a particular way to do a particular work. I do not always experience physical phenomena when God is speaking, but on this occasion I did and it was helpful in recognizing God's activity.

The "knowing" that words for physical healing were coming is not so easy to describe, but it is a common, everyday experience for many people. It is no different from ordinary premonitions such as, "I knew this was going to happen" or "I sensed my mother was ill" or "I just felt it in my bones." Outside the "religious experience" arena we frequently talk of hunches, intuitions, or uncanny feelings, and my "knowing" seemed no different from these.

The words in my mind came like thinking through a problem or making things up out of my imagination. People looking for words from the Spirit often look for something apart from themselves or outside their normal experience, but the Holy Spirit *indwells* the believer, enabling us to develop the mind of Christ, who is in us as we are in Him. Satan's demons seek to possess us, but the Spirit of God comes to free us that we might become more truly ourselves. Serious religious people frequently find that the Spirit speaks to them in serious tones, while those with a sharp sense of humor commonly find the Spirit has the last laugh. I believe we need to look for the Holy Spirit most often within our experience rather than outside it.

After I had thought about the five parts of the body, I pointed out to God there was rather insufficient detail for a meeting of about ninety people. From then on the thinking followed a question and answer pattern that went something like this:

"Tell me more about this big toe on the right foot."

"It's a man with an ingrowing toenail that is black and blue."

"But, Lord, I suffer from an ingrowing toenail and it never goes black and blue."

Silence.

"What about the bowels then?"

"A lady with a serious bowel complaint, who has had the problem for some time."

"What is the problem with the chest?"

"Interventricular."

(This was very odd. It's always worth noting unusual words, particularly as I didn't think I'd ever heard this one before.) I thought it was for a lady and had something to do with the lungs.

"The mouth?"

"Mouth ulcer."

"What gender?"

Silence.

"The head?"

"A severe headache."

"Anything more?"

"It's time for the funeral."

I looked at my watch and rushed into the chapel just in time. It wasn't the easiest cremation I'd ever done, but I saw it through as sensitively as I could and then went home.

At first I was too embarrassed to share the words I'd received with Carol. It felt as though I'd been playing a silly game, pretending to be some superspiritual giant who could hear God, and I needed to remind myself of my own sermon: "Our God is a God who speaks and lives in every believer." Encouraged, but still very much afraid, I reached for the dictionary and was overjoyed to find that "ventricular" really was a word, but concerning the heart rather than the lungs.

Tackling Cynicism

I decided to tackle head-on the problem of giving words from the Spirit to a Church of England congregation. People tend to creep up afterward and say, "That word was for me, but I didn't like to claim it in front of all these people." I decided to tell them about the bishop and the man with the thumb, and how I felt about it at the time. I would then give all the words at once, before asking everyone to come forward together. That seemed fine, but supposing they were there and did come forward, what would I do next?

"Lord," I said, hoping He hadn't given up on me, "the people I'm taking with me from our own church have even less clue than I do; how shall we pray?" Again the thoughts in my head felt a little like having a conversation with myself: "The big toe is not the man's main problem; minister as led. The bowel problem is serious. The heart is a physical problem I want to heal. The mouth ulcer is something more than that, and the headache will be healed by laying hands on the back."

Eventually I plucked up the courage to share all this information with Carol, who appreciated my fears. "You'll get loads of mouth ulcers," she said. "I've got one myself at present."

We arrived at ten to eight to find nobody there except the music group, so we slipped into a back room to pray. I had a bad throat. It was January. Greg then told me I would be fine by the time I got up to speak, and I was, not even needing a glass of water.

As I stood at the side during worship, a deep peace came over me. The previous six hours had been a mixture of excitement and paralyzing fear, but now the presence of God took over and I knew all I had was from Him. From then on the proceedings felt like acting out something already written. With hindsight I believe this was the Spirit's gift of faith (1 Cor. 12:9).

I preached about the God who speaks, shared how important it was to claim words from Him when given, and then gave out my five words. As I gave the word about the toe, Charles looked at his wife in disbelief. While at work that afternoon he banged the toe on his right foot, which aggravated his ingrowing toenail problem. He called his wife into the bathroom at six o'clock to look at his black and blue nail as he tackled it with scissors. When I gave the word about the toe, a lady was saying to herself, "I bet there are loads of people here with bad toes." Two years previously she'd narrowly avoided a very serious bowel operation and had been lucky to survive. She knew the second word, when it came, was for her.

While all this was going on, Jan Coleman was in agony. Two or three times a week she suffered from very painful palpitations due to a damaged left ventricle, and she was having one at the time. This is Jan's account of what happened:

> Towards the end of the last song before the ministry began, the palpitations started and so did the chest pain, which became quite severe—legs were trembling and weakness spread throughout my body. No one else in the church knew that I was actually having an attack then, but a few friends knew of the problem. I slumped into the chair in the hope that no one would notice what was happening to me, also because my physical strength seemed to desert me. When Peter gave the word "inter-ventricular," it was as if God was calling me by name. I was upset that he had allowed this to happen in church and started to weep. Several people who knew I had this complaint reached towards me and said, "That's you, Jan, go on." Although my desire was to hide—I didn't want to be exposed—I couldn't fight it and it was not with my own strength that I rose and struggled forward. I was really surprised when I found myself heading towards the front of the church.

I mentioned the mouth ulcer and headache, and everyone assembled at the front. There were three people claiming bad headaches so I said to the first man, "I thought the Lord was saying the headache would be healed by laying hands on the back." He laughed. The day before a specialist had diagnosed that his severe permanent headache came from a form of rheumatism in the spine.

When people laid hands on Jan Coleman, power seemed to go right across her chest and her heart stopped beating. *I'm dead*, she thought, but upon opening her eyes and seeing she was still in an Anglican church, not heaven, she realized it was just the palpitations stopping. Jan hasn't had any palpitations since that night. She was our first healing, set up by the Holy Spirit as He spoke words to us.

The lady for whom Sarah prayed, who claimed the word about the serious bowel complaint, kindly sent me the following account:

> I went to this meeting somewhat wary of the whole basis of the "Signs and Wonders" ministry, having read a book critical of it. Hence I was not especially expectant.
>
> During the meeting Peter mentioned various ailments which he believed God was revealing to him, as being suffered by particular people present. Some of these were very specific, including one which related to my own condition. Had it been a very vague description, I would not have gone forward for prayer.
>
> I went to a side room with a young girl from Peter's team. She said it was the first time she had ever done this sort of thing so, coupled with my own neutral if not negative feelings about the whole procedure, this did not seem to bode well.

She prayed one very short and simple prayer and so did I. To my surprise I experienced a very sudden inrushing of the Spirit, creating a physical sensation I have only experienced twice before in the last fifteen years. It was very powerful, though lasting only a couple of minutes.

It must be said that this lady did not experience physical healing that night. God had told me it was serious, nothing more; but at least now He had her attention.

Afterward Charles scribbled down what happened to him. This is what he wrote:

> I was an original doubting Thomas, I did not believe God spoke to people directly. However, that Thursday night was the start for me to seek a new and much deeper relationship with God. If God cared enough to use my bruised big toe to speak to me, then how much more I needed to listen to him speak directly to me about how I lived my whole life.... I did not start to grow as a Christian until I listened to God speak directly to me.

Andrew was the only one to claim a mouth ulcer, and he felt he had to come forward after what I'd said in my sermon about claiming the Spirit's words. He had some doubts about charismatic Christianity before that night.

The man with rheumatism had a back and neck problem rather than just a severe headache. Following ministry that night, he later testified that since then the headache problem has occurred less frequently. He began to go regularly for prayer at the church's own healing services.

The experienced eye will probably discern how God seemed to be healing cynicism and disbelief that night as much as bodies—not least my own. I have heard some people describe words from the Spirit as mere psychic impulses that some receive when they are in the same room as the sick or needy person. I can only say that on several occasions besides this one, the Spirit has graciously given me words well in advance of meetings, helping me to avoid the intrusion of my own thoughts. I cannot believe that receiving words at a quarter to two in the afternoon for an evening meeting, about people I had never met before, could be interpreted as psychic impulses. Especially as one person had suffered for over two years, two for several months, one only quite recently, and one had not yet banged his toe when I received the word about it.

We prayed for them in the name of Jesus and no other name, so it is inappropriate to suspect that the information had a demonic source. As far as I am concerned, the Spirit Himself validated the claim that He is a God who speaks.

According to the Bible, the God and Father of our Lord Jesus Christ is a God who speaks and lives inside every born-again Christian by His Spirit. If the God who speaks lives inside every believer, then I believe, from time to time, we should all expect Him to speak to us by His Spirit. The Word of God gives us this expectation. In my experience it is this expectation, built on the solid rock of Scripture, that so often makes the difference between hearing the Spirit speak and not hearing Him. We are not all going to get words from God for other people, and certainly not every day, but we should expect to be in communication with the Spirit more and more as we attune our own spiritual ears to His voice.

My experience at that church, following my study of the Bible, was something of a watershed moment for me, and I'm delighted to say the Holy Spirit has often turned up since. The five words from God seemed to confirm to me that our God is a God who speaks.

3

THE ADVENTURE OF PRAYER

Before I attended John Wimber's meetings at Sheffield, I considered prayer something of a chore and a lifeless discipline. I brought along my agenda and shopping list, said "Amen," and got up to go without waiting for an answer. But now that I had met the Spirit who speaks, I began to discover the thrill and the adventure of prayer in God's response.

Often we are so busy doing, we never have any time for being. When we look for God, we normally seek His hand rather than His face: what He can do for us rather than who He is. Prayer is useful; it can get things done. We think the purpose of prayer is life. But when I read of Jesus' prayers in the Gospels—His intimate relationship with His Father—everything turned upside down. For Jesus, the purpose of life seems to be prayer. If the end of this life is the gateway to an eternity spent enjoying God face-to-face and worshipping Him, then maybe prayer is not the necessary chore that leads to a more fulfilled and "successful" Christian life, but the ultimate goal toward which we are striving.

Our group of young people continued to meet with me on Sunday nights, and these little gatherings became an experiment in prayer. We continued praying for people and needs, petitioning God in the traditional way, but we also made room for God to come and speak, minister, or do whatever He wanted to do. We would sit, eyes closed, welcome Him, and then wait.

On one evening at about nine thirty, the young people and I began waiting upon God, and gradually those present experienced the power of the Holy Spirit. Some felt heat, a few started shaking gently, and one young man slid off his chair onto the floor, where he stayed beaming for some time. People laid hands on one another and together we shared God's love. By ten o'clock everything had died down and the meeting dispersed as the youngsters and leaders made their way home, all that is, except Jo.

As everyone else gathered their belongings and left, Jo remained seated, eyes closed, with her hands together on her lap. Her Christian parents arrived to take her home in the car, but chose to wait as they also sensed something more important than an early night's sleep was taking place. We tried laying hands on her and blessing what the Father was doing, but nothing we did made any difference, so eventually we just sat, watching and waiting.

At ten thirty I quietly asked God what was happening, and the idea formed in my mind that Jo was having a vision and not to interfere. Five minutes later her hands separated, the palms turned upward, and she slowly lifted her arms. Her left hand began to shake (she is left-handed), and one solitary tear made its way down her face. At five to eleven I felt God telling me to prepare pen and paper to write down what Jo had seen, and at eleven o'clock she opened her eyes.

"What's been happening, Jo?" I asked gently.

"You've no idea," she began falteringly. "You've no idea how much God loves us."

It seemed strange that a sixteen-year-old girl should be saying this to a middle-aged vicar, but it was true. This is what we wrote down:

> At first it was as if I was physically bolted to the floor. Then I felt I was being lifted up—transported past pillars of silver. I could see the colours of the rainbow and there was a very bright light around all the time. I saw the side of a golden throne, but the light seemed to prevent me seeing the whole of it. There were steps leading up to the throne and in my vision I fell down—it was so powerful. I was still in the light when I saw through the shape of an eye the cross and Jesus. The feeling of love was tremendous. God's love and power was overwhelming; it just cannot be described adequately.

I should clarify that Jo is not a very emotional person. She had struggled with God all day, as nothing ever happened to her, and was amazed when I later showed her the rainbows described in Ezekiel and Revelation: She did not know the rainbow she saw was in Scripture. When her friends at school asked her how she had spent Sunday, they did not expect to hear that Jo had spent an hour and a half with God, or that it was one of the most exciting times of her life.

The New Covenant Promise of God

Jeremiah records this prophecy:

> "The time is coming," declares the LORD,
>   "when I will make a new covenant
> with the house of Israel
>   and with the house of Judah....
> This is the covenant that I will make with the house of
>   Israel
>   after that time," declares the LORD.
> "I will put my law in their minds
>   and write it on their hearts.
> I will be their God,
>   and they will be my people.
> No longer will a man teach his neighbor,
>   or a man his brother, saying, 'Know the LORD,'
> because they will all know me,
>   from the least of them to the greatest."
>   (Jer. 31:31–34; see also Heb. 8:8–12)

This is the new covenant promise of God to His people. Jeremiah declares the old covenant has been broken (Jer. 31:32), but a new one is coming, and this is the solemn promise of God. "I will put my law in their minds and write it on their hearts. I will be their God, and they will be my people" (Jer. 31:33). The result of this is, "they will all know me, from the least of them to the greatest" (Jer. 31:34).

God made His new covenant with the Jews through the Jew Jesus and explained it with twelve representative Jews present at the

Last Supper, but the Gentiles who believe in Jesus are also grafted in. The promise is for them too—all who believe in Jesus (Rom. 11:11–24).

This is some promise! Instead of a set of laws written on tablets of stone, God is going to make His will known by writing it on people's minds and hearts. And this is not just for special individuals; all His people who enter the new covenant through Jesus, from the least to the greatest, will know the Spirit who speaks. Under the old covenant, chosen people such as prophets spoke with the guidance of the Holy Spirit, but under the new covenant, this promise is for all believers—Jews and Gentiles (Acts 2:38–39).

Jesus saw Himself as the fulfiller of this new covenant promise: "This cup is the new covenant in my blood, which is poured out for you," he said (Luke 22:20; cf. Matt. 26:28; Mark 14:24; 1 Cor. 11:25). Hebrews chapters 8 and 9 explain it more fully. The death of Christ on the cross opens the door of the new covenant from God's side, and all who believe in Jesus and receive His sacrifice enter a new covenant relationship with God through that door. The death of Christ enables us to be right with God, and the Holy Spirit seals the deal.

Jesus explains how it comes about:

> I will ask the Father, and he will give you another Counselor to be with you forever—the Spirit of truth. The world cannot accept him, because it neither sees him nor knows him. But you know him, for he lives with you and will be in you.… On that day you will realize that I am in my Father, and you are in me, and I am in you. (John 14:16–17, 20)

Jesus says the Holy Spirit will be in us and will teach us all things. He will give us the mind of Christ and enable us to know God on the inside—just as Jeremiah prophesied (John 14:26). Although Jesus addressed those words to His close disciples, the New Testament writers believed this promise came true at Pentecost for all who trust in Jesus (Acts 2:38–39). They believed the Holy Spirit is available to all believers:

"If anyone acknowledges that Jesus is the Son of God, God lives in him and he in God" (1 John 4:15).

"We know that we live in him and he in us, because he has given us of his Spirit" (1 John 4:13).

"Don't you know that you yourselves are God's temple and that God's Spirit lives in you?" (1 Cor. 3:16).

The early Christians experienced several external communications from God, such as the occasional angel or voice from heaven, but they seemed to be even more familiar with the Holy Spirit who lived inside each one. The Holy Spirit often spoke to them:

"The Spirit told Philip, 'Go to that chariot'" (Acts 8:29).

"While Peter was still thinking about the vision, the Spirit said to him …" (Acts 10:19).

Agabus "stood up and through the Spirit predicted … a severe famine" (Acts 11:28).

"The Holy Spirit said, 'Set apart for me Barnabas and Saul'" (Acts 13:2).

I believe these verses refer to the inner prompting or "knowing" about which Jeremiah, Jesus, and Paul spoke (Jer. 31:34; John 14:17; Rom. 8:9).

The Bible describes external encounters with the living God who brings messages to His people, as when Mary met the angel

Gabriel, but He never promises these encounters will occur. They may happen, and indeed they do happen, but Scripture does not say we can expect them to happen to everyone. God does not promise blinding lights and flames of fire to all who turn to Him, but He does promise to give us a new heart and put a new spirit within us (Ezek. 36:26). Jesus does not say that when He has gone to the Father He will send legions of angels to give us our daily instructions, but He promises to send the Spirit that we may be in Him, and He in us (John 14:16–17). The Spirit does not guarantee to write words on walls, tablets of stone, or people's foreheads, but to write His truth in our minds (Heb. 8:10). God gives His Holy Spirit to all believers. They can expect to hear Him and know Him within their innermost being, and I believe that is where we should look regularly for God's direct communication to us. It is this inner experience of God by the Holy Spirit, the Spirit of Jesus, that the Bible promises to all believers.

Paul writes in Romans that every Jew and every Gentile with faith in Jesus has the Spirit of Him who raised Jesus from the dead (Rom. 8:9–11). If the God who loves to speak to us lives inside us, it is obvious that, from time to time, we can expect Him to speak. It is the promise of Scripture.

An Urgent Command

One winter, deep snow greatly affected church attendance; all the major roads were still open, but everyone was advised to stay indoors except for emergencies. Monday was my day off, the schools were closed, nobody would expect me to visit them, and I could stay in bed or spend the day playing with our children.

God, of course, doesn't take Mondays off, and I awoke at eight o'clock with a sense of urgency all over me. "Lord, why do I feel like this?" I prayed while still in bed. The answering thought in my mind was instant: "Get up immediately. I want you to go and visit Rose in hospital right now."

This was not only an unwelcome idea but a very impractical one, as my garage was built on a steep, narrow incline. My car had not been out for days, the door and drive were blocked with four or five feet of snow, and the hospital was several miles away.

Carol smiled and kissed me on my way as I took giant steps in my wellies and made deep holes in the crusty ice to steady myself as I went. During the night a fierce wind had swept large drifts against the garage door, and as I began to dig for God, several local teenagers recognized my clerical collar and gathered to jeer me on. The car was surprised to see me and reluctant to start, but after considerable revving we rushed backward together down the slope, slid narrowly past the wall, and skidded to a halt inches from the nearby tree. The youngsters' jeers turned to cheers as they witnessed my spectacular slalom descent, and they waved me on my journey as I made it slowly and safely to the hospital. The parking lot was almost totally deserted when I arrived.

I was at Rose's side by half past nine, with the curtains drawn around her bed, and very quickly assessed the situation. Rose, a faithful eighty-four-year-old member of our congregation, was unconscious and struggling for breath. I was distressed to see her in this condition, and I didn't know what to do. The suggestion "pray in tongues" formed in my mind, which I did for a few minutes, and was about to stop when the words "keep going" encouraged me to persist.

After about fifteen minutes the atmosphere changed, light came into the area, power and heat came on my body, and this thought came to me: "Now you can lay hands on Rose." I did so gently, experiencing tingling sensations that came through my hands, and the distress in Jesus' faithful servant gave way to peace. I prayed my best prayers in English, committed Rose into the hands of God, and then stayed put for a further five minutes.

An incredible stillness surrounded me and I didn't want to leave. "You've finished now," came the thought. "You can go," but in truth it felt as if heaven had broken in and I wanted to stay and worship. Despite experiencing an electric and awesome presence, I obeyed the prompting and made my way slowly back to the car. With God's help I completed the return journey home, up the slope, and into the garage totally unscathed.

I was building a snowman in the garden with our girls when Rose's daughter rang me. When the family arrived at the hospital at ten o'clock, Rose was already dead. After I told them what had happened, they were sad but very relieved. They also gave me permission to tell the story at the funeral as an example of God's love and care for Rose, even at the end. I cannot say why God wanted me to be present and to pray before Rose died; maybe in some way it eased her passing, but whatever the reason I felt sure my sense of urgency and the message I received came from the Holy Spirit who lives inside me.

Finding God's Voice in Provable Situations

To those who want to hear a word or a prophecy from the Holy Spirit, I always say, "Ask the Lord to give you a word that can be provably right or provably wrong; that is how we begin to hear the voice of God." When it isn't clear if we are wrong or right, then we must begin to discover if God is speaking to us by checking things out as we go along. When we have done this a few times, we can ask to give prophecies or words in groups or in church.

So often in "charismatic" churches people give prophecies that cannot be checked or found to be demonstrably right or wrong. Those optimistic in nature often speak about waves that are coming, revival approaching, or healings and signs soon filling the church. Those who are pessimistic speak about the need for more repentance or say that God is judging us and the church is not what it ought to be. A third group inevitably prophesies about the pastor or the leadership or the way they could run the church much better themselves, if given the chance. So much "prophecy" in churches sounds to me like people's own ideas wrapped up in religious language. But if we start by asking God to give us words that can be tested in the light of what actually happens, it helps determine if our words are from the Holy Spirit or from our own fertile imaginations and adds a measure of objectivity to the process. For example:

Peter discerned in the Spirit that Ananias and Sapphira had lied (Acts 5). He knew he was right when they dropped down dead.

"The Spirit told Philip, 'Go to that chariot and stay near it'" (Acts 8:29). Philip knew it was the Spirit because the Ethiopian was reading Isaiah 53 and was baptized almost instantaneously.

Ananias (not the one that dropped down dead) saw a vision and was told to go to the house of Judas on Straight Street (Acts 9). He knew it was the Spirit because Paul was there.

The Lord told Paul that Elymas would be blind (Acts 13). Paul knew it was the Spirit when Elymas became blind.

Peter, Philip, Ananias, and Paul knew it was the Holy Spirit who spoke to them because the words were provably—and proved to be—accurate.

I was driving home one day at about four o'clock in the afternoon, looking forward to seeing Carol and our children, when I found myself driving past Angela's house. Angela was a sixteen-year-old member of our church who lived at home with her mother; her father had died a couple of years before. Seeing her house reminded me that I wanted to see her about something to do with our youth club.

I stopped the car at the side of the road and was about to get out when I remembered that Angela didn't go to school locally and didn't get home until five o'clock. I looked at the house for any sign of life, such as a window open or a light on, but there was nothing to challenge my second thoughts. I was about to start up the car when a further thought entered my head: "Angela is there, go and knock on the door."

Only a Christian who believes the Holy Spirit lives inside each believer, only one who has realized the Bible rests on the assumption that God speaks, only one familiar with the biographies of other Christians and the saints of old, would pay attention to a thought like this at the side of the road at teatime.

In George Bernard Shaw's play *Saint Joan,* the newly crowned King Charles has this conversation with Joan of Arc:

> CHARLES: Oh, your voices, your voices. Why don't
> the voices come to me? I am king, not you.

JOAN: They do come to you; but you do not hear
them. You have not sat in the field in the evening
listening for them. When the angelus rings you
cross yourself and have done with it; but if you
prayed from your heart, and listened to the thrilling
of the bells in the air after they stop ringing, you
would hear the voices as well as I do.[1]

There were not many of St. Joan's fields readily available in
inner-city Birmingham, so I sat in the car by the side of the road and
tried to reason things out. It was not a logical thought so, despite the
truths of the Bible, I still had a something of a spiritual struggle. I am
British, after all. The house looked unoccupied and I knew Angela
did not normally come home until five o'clock.

*But there is nothing to lose. If she's not there I simply knock at the
door, wait, and walk away.*

*But I don't live my life based on random thoughts, but sensible
propositions and plans.*

But God lives inside me. He knows what I don't know.

I paused, wrestled a bit more, then eventually gave in with the
thought that nobody would know and I wouldn't look foolish. I
slowly got out of the car, locked it carefully, went down the path, and
rang the bell. Angela came to the door in her school uniform.

"How did you know I was here?" she responded sheepishly. "I
skived off the last lesson from school."

"God told me," I said. Her admission of guilt confirmed my
thoughts; she could easily have assumed I was visiting her mother.
The next sentence, however, was also very important.

"Mother's here," she said. "Come in."

If Jesus could hear Satan speaking in the desert, then I could hear him or his minions at the side of the road. If Angela had come to the door with a bath towel draped loosely around her, flashed her eyelashes at me, and said, "Hello, Peter darling. How nice to see you. Mother won't be back for hours, do come in," I may have been in possession of supernatural knowledge, but not from the Holy Spirit. Mother, however, was in and Angela was here fully dressed.

The three of us chatted in the back room over tea and cake, and I quickly discovered what I needed to know about the youth club. Mother then listened while I shared with her daughter some of the exciting things about the movement of the Holy Spirit taking place among our youngsters. Being very traditional in her churchgoing, she was absolutely fascinated to hear what was happening and pleased to know that her only child was now embracing the Christian faith for herself.

Later they took out one of Uncle George's ukuleles for me. Uncle George was none other than George Formby, a popular entertainer between the two world wars. They showed me some photographs of him with Angela's father, and I realized how helpful it was for both of them to talk about the man in their lives who was now missing. It was an encounter that Angela's uncle would have said had "turned out nice"—with a smile.

The Value of Listening with Others

The Bible assures us that everybody under the new covenant has the Spirit of God living within and can hear God speak. This means that when believers come together, we can know the will of God for our churches, but it isn't easy. Hearing God on our own is one thing; doing so with others is quite another. Therefore we need to clarify from the beginning what we are trying to do and why.

Whenever I hear sermons or teaching on the topic of the church, the preachers invariably mention the similes and figures of speech used in the New Testament:

The church is *like* a body—"we are all members of one body" (Eph. 4:25).

We are *like* living stones—"being built into a spiritual house" (1 Peter 2:5).

We are *like* a household (Eph. 2:19)—a temple (2 Cor. 6:16)—a family (Eph. 3:15).

Church teachers love analogies and figures of speech, but if we want to know what the New Testament church was in reality—we need to know not what the church of Christ was *like,* but what it *was.*

In the Gospels, Jesus told the disciples what to do. If Jesus said they were going to Jerusalem, to a mountain, going sailing, or going home, they all went. If Jesus told them to go in pairs to proclaim the kingdom of God, heal the sick, and cast out demons, they did it (Luke 9:2). Wherever Jesus went, they went, and whatever they were told to do, they did.

The early church in the New Testament continued this process of doing what Jesus was doing. In Acts the church is the community of the Holy Spirit—the Spirit of Jesus. Whatever Jesus told them to do, by His Spirit, they did. They sought to hear Him and to obey Him. The church of Christ was the followers of Jesus doing what He told them to do as He spoke in the flesh in the Gospels and in the Spirit in Acts.

This is also the principle found in the Epistles. Although Jesus had ascended into heaven, whatever the Spirit of Jesus said to the church—they did. Some of the teaching in the New Testament may resemble figures of speech, but the church of Christ really was the followers of Jesus doing what He told them to do. This they did more or less successfully, and the principle continued throughout the New Testament.

Consider the following verses, all underlining the basic truth that the Holy Spirit gives us access to the Father through Jesus.

> While they were worshiping the Lord and fasting, the Holy Spirit said, "Set apart for me Barnabas and Saul for the work to which I have called them." So after they had fasted and prayed, they placed their hands on them and sent them off. (Acts 13:2–3)

> He who has an ear, let him hear what the Spirit says to the churches. (Rev. 2:7)

> Those who are led by the Spirit of God are sons of God. (Rom. 8:14)

> We have the mind of Christ. (1 Cor. 2:16)

> Since we live by the Spirit, let us keep in step with the Spirit. (Gal. 5:25)

> For through him we both have access to the Father by one Spirit. (Eph. 2:18)

God ... [gives] gifts of the Holy Spirit distributed
according to his will. (Heb. 2:4)

You are blessed, for the Spirit of glory and of God
rests on you. (1 Peter 4:14)

This is how we know that he lives in us: We know it
by the Spirit he gave us. (1 John 3:24)

We know that we live in him and he in us, because
he has given us of his Spirit. (1 John 4:13)

The New Testament teaching of Jesus and of those who knew
Him is the doctrine of the church. But day-to-day guidance is what
the Holy Spirit gives in order for us to do what Jesus wants us to
do. The church is made up of those who have been born again by
the Spirit, and each person, from the least to the greatest, has the
Holy Spirit inside him or her. The church of Christ is therefore the
community of the Spirit—motivated by doing the will of Jesus and
seeking to discover the voice of the Spirit on earth for the purpose of
obeying Him. Everything else about the church of Christ on earth is
of secondary importance.

Sadly, the majority of the churches in the West do not function
this way.

Twenty-two years after the "Signs and Wonders" conference in
Sheffield, I was invited to a church to lead a day focused on "the
Spirit who heals." As we were worshipping in song at the begin-
ning of the afternoon session, the power of the Holy Spirit came

upon me. Since it was a Methodist church, it is probably appropriate to record that, in the tradition of Mr. Wesley, I felt "strangely warmed."[2]

I sat down immediately and asked the Lord to show me why He was calling. At once, with my eyes closed, I saw in a vision the silhouette of a lady. I could not make out the details of nose, mouth, or clothing, but the shape was very distinctive. With my eyes still closed, I asked the Lord what it meant and some words formed in my mind.

"The lady has something wrong with her eyes and the right one is worse than the left," He seemed to say.

"Thank you, Lord," I replied. "And what shall I do with this word?"

"Give it out when you get up to speak this afternoon," He said, "and ask Carol and Gill to minister to her while everyone else watches."

This is the challenge of the prayer of faith. There is not always any way of knowing beforehand if the word is correct or if anything will happen. The right response to God, if it is God, requires a mixture of obedience, faith, and willingness to be a fool for Christ. Whenever I try to help others overcome this hurdle, I frequently ask them three questions:

1. If the word is right and the person is healed, who gets all the glory? Answer: Jesus.
2. If the word is wrong and nothing happens, who gets all the blame? Answer: I do.
3. So what's stopping me? Answer: My ego, or my fear.

My aim is to always be obedient to the Spirit and advance the kingdom of God, on earth as in heaven. Praying publicly for people, however, while the congregation watches, is not an easy thing to do and may not always be helpful or advisable. I always ask for sensitivity and sometimes a "word of wisdom" before doing this.

As I stood up to speak, I gave out the word and asked if anyone among the forty people present felt it was for them. Margaret was sitting at the back because she is a delightfully shy, reserved lady, but she felt the word was too "correct" to ignore and bravely stood up. At once I saw before me the exact representation of the silhouette in my mind's eye, albeit much more complete with the details filled in. Margaret did indeed have something wrong with both eyes; yes the right eye was much worse than the left; and yes she would come forward to receive prayer.

My wife, Carol, and friend Gill gently laid hands on Margaret; I asked God the Father through Jesus to send His Holy Spirit on her, and He came. Slowly, gently, she crumpled forward and then lay down on the floor while Carol and Gill knelt down beside her and carried on ministering until the Spirit had finished. I carried on speaking, since nobody but the front row could now see what was happening.

On the following Wednesday, Margaret kept an appointment with her optician, who told her both eyes were now normal. I received a letter with these comments a little while later.

> I just wanted to write a personal "thank you" for
> last weekend, which will rate as one of the most

special times of my life. I have to admit, although I've been present at similar occasions, I've always felt rather "distant" at the times of ministry.

So the way the Spirit came on me so powerfully last weekend, was completely overwhelming, and a tremendous blessing. I had a "follow-up" visit to my optician this last week … she was quite satisfied that the test I had on Wednesday was showing the eye was "normal." As she is a Christian, I was able to share that I received prayer for healing and she could identify with that, as she had experienced such prayer.

To God be the glory!

Helping One Another to Get Going

The so-called Enlightenment has greatly influenced our Western mind-set, leading to widespread secularization in modern-day culture. Consequently we do not find it easy to hear from God. So I often use spiritual exercises, based on 1 Corinthians 12:8–10 and supported by prayer, which may help others to get going. This is what I typically do in our church, house groups, and other gatherings.

Part 1: The First Session

A. In groups of about six to eight we appoint a leader. Everyone has the opportunity to take part if they wish to do so.

B. The leader starts by saying something biblical about God and everyone is encouraged to do the same, maybe each one in turn. Something like "God is love."

C. We repeat the process—e.g., "God is forgiving." The aim is to start with something that everyone can do but also to establish a language framework into which words from God will fit.

D. The leader now demonstrates how to turn a statement about God into a word from God—and how to speak on behalf of God. So—"God is love" becomes "I love you, My children," and "God is forgiving" becomes "I forgive you, My children." If possible, everyone in the group turns one of their statements about God into a word from God.

E. Now we move from theory into reality. The leader asks God, through Jesus, to send His Holy Spirit upon us, so that everyone might receive and give a word from God that He wants to say to the group. We wait for each person in turn to receive a word and then go round the group, sharing what we believe God wants to say to us. It may be that some will say something generally true like "I love you, My children," but one or two will quite likely come out with something more specific, like "I feel the Lord is saying that He wants the members of this group to learn to trust one

another before sharing what we are doing with
the wider church." (Either way, whether the word
is general or specific, the leader will need to check
that everything said accords with biblical truth.)

For many people this may be enough for the first session. The
leader will need to gauge how far people can go based on their past
experiences of the gifts of the Spirit, how far outside their comfort
zone this is, and whether anything unbiblical or inappropriate was
offered as a word in this first try. At this point it doesn't matter if the
words are biblical truths or personal messages, as long as the content
is scriptural. Nor does every person in the group need to be mature,
either in years or in Christian experience. While the fruit of the Spirit
usually grows slowly, the gifts are often evident in new Christians,
old and young.

This first session finishes after the leader encourages the members
to claim any of the prophecies or asks if a word has spoken to anyone
in particular. It may also be good to turn some of the prophecies into
prayers.

Part 2: The Intermediate Session

A. This may be days later, or it could be several
weeks—so much depends on the people and
how comfortable they are with this. The leader
asks God the Father, through Jesus, to send the
Holy Spirit to give "words of knowledge" to the
group. We wait until everyone is ready and then

either go round the group or ask if anyone has a word. Normally we give the word without saying whom it may be for and ask if it means anything to anyone. The leader may need to encourage everyone to claim words so that we will know if a word is right or wrong. If words are claimed, it may be right for the group to pray for everyone who claims one, perhaps adding other words as it seems right to the group and to the Holy Spirit. The leader may need to teach that words are sometimes partially right, or that the same word may be appropriate for more than one person at a time.

B. If God seems to be giving a tricky word, then we may also need a "word of wisdom." Alternatively, if somebody offers an embarrassing word, the leader may need to step in and suggest that if anyone thinks it's for them, they may prefer to speak to the person privately, or to the leader or pastor afterward. It is, however, a great encouragement to the person who gave the word if they know at some stage that it was right.

C. The leader then asks the Holy Spirit to give messages in tongues. If this happens, the leader asks the Holy Spirit to give the interpretation, and once more the group weighs the words and responds. At the very least, if the group receives any words, they should be turned into prayers.

Part 3: The Advanced Session

A. The leader asks God the Father, through Jesus, to
    send the Holy Spirit to do whatever He wants to
    do. If God then gives faith for healing, or mira-
    cles, or to deal with anything demonic that may
    be causing trouble, we pray accordingly, or minis-
    ter to individuals as the Lord leads. Frequently we
    pray for those who need to be healed.

In my experience, taking part in such spiritual exercises tends to
work best when we cover the whole activity with prayer. Then, when
God breaks in among us, hearing a word from Him can be a life-
changing experience for individuals, the group, and the church. Most
of us are thrilled when God speaks to us, and I never tire of experiencing the buzz during coffee after God has spoken to His people.

On one occasion Bruce Collins led a New Wine conference at
our church. He encouraged us to get into small groups and ask the
Holy Spirit to give us words for one another. As we waited on the
Holy Spirit, I wondered if God was saying to me that one of the
people present had a few physical problems, so I shared my thoughts
with the group. An elderly lady asked me if I would pray for her
privately, and I was happy to do so.

The Holy Spirit then seemed to say the problem had arisen
since she had been bereaved, and she confirmed this was the case.
As I prayed for her, the Holy Spirit came upon her powerfully, but
what really stayed with her all day, along with some alleviation of her
symptoms, was that Jesus had spoken to her.

God came to her and spoke to her in her bereaved state—not something that had happened to her before—and it changed her. When Bruce took the chance of letting the Holy Spirit give us words for each other, a struggling, not-very-well, bereaved widow felt greatly loved by God.

Some teachers or writers like categorizing or providing lists of the ways God can speak to us. Telling people stories about the variety of ways God might speak certainly makes the teacher look good. But in my experience it is more helpful to do it than to talk about it. Asking the Father to send His Holy Spirit upon us to speak to us as individuals and churches is normally all we need, along with the determination to listen, because God loves to speak to us. It is the promise of Scripture that if we ask Him to come, wait for Him to come, and respond to His coming … He will come (Luke 11:9–13).

4

PROCLAIM THE KING
AND THE KINGDOM

Taking It to the Streets

"We want more in-depth teaching," people cry. "More time set aside to discuss and study the profound hidden truths of Scripture, more *meat*, less *milk*." And whenever they called out in need to John Wimber, he would reply, "The meat is on the street." Satisfying the intellect, organizing navel-gazing sessions of *Veni Sancte Spiritus,* and stuffing faces with more and more introspective, hedonistic, spiritual pleasures, was not what John was talking about. Jesus took signs and wonders out onto the street; the early church took signs and wonders out onto the street; and so did John Wimber.

We tried it too, but it didn't work very well. Not at first, anyway.

Many of the local youths who lived in inner-city Birmingham had criminal records. On several occasions we tried praying for them, but nothing ever happened, until one day my friends Derek and Norma invited me to meet their young people. They were youth workers, and I went to speak to them, but when I arrived at their small terraced house, in a rough part of town, there were no young people present. "Where's the youth group?" I asked.

"We don't have a youth group as such," explained Derek. "We just go out on the streets on Friday nights and invite anyone we see to come in for coffee."

"Oh!" I said. "Right."

After going out the first time, they returned with two girls aged about ten and a fourteen-year-old boy, and over coffee I shared a few healing stories. As soon as the hot drinks were consumed, however, they all got up and left.

Not going well, I thought, and rather hoped they wouldn't come back. But they did—with four older teenage lads of considerable size, decked out in ferocious-looking leather gear, and all wearing earrings. I shared a few more stories with them, and once more the two girls got up and walked out (it was now time for them to go home). Only this time the five teenage lads remained behind to drink more coffee.

I must say I felt like a flapping fish out of water, and was ready to thank Derek and Norma for their hospitality and make my own excuses, when an uncomfortable kind of "knowing" spread all over me. The Spirit who speaks seemed to be at it again, and I sensed that if I offered "ministry" rather than just "talk," something would happen. I wondered why this should be any different from the failures we experienced with our own streetwise kids. I thought it through briefly and came to these conclusions.

1. These lads didn't know me, and I was not in my own parish.

2. I therefore had nothing to lose.
3. If I asked the Holy Spirit to come, it was His responsibility, not mine.

Having found no valid excuse for running away, I went for it.

"Shall we ask God to send His Holy Spirit on us?" I inquired.

"What, now?" one of them protested.

I prayed for help silently, urgently, and another word from the Holy Spirit popped up—a word of wisdom (1 Cor. 12:8 NKJV), something to unlock the moment.

"You're not chicken, are you?" I challenged.

"Chicken!" they all exclaimed together. "No. We're not chicken."

"Go on then," the ringleader said.

Then, in a very small kitchen, four large, mean-looking, leather-jacketed tough-guys with earrings stood up—along with the fourteen-year-old lad who had stayed with them—closed their eyes, and held out their hands, as I instructed. Then I prayed, "Come, Holy Spirit."

After a few moments they laughed nervously and loudly. Reaching deep into my past experiences as a schoolteacher, I rebuked them, quieted everything down, and slowly the Spirit came on them all.

One by one four of them fell face down onto the kitchen floor, where they remained in a motionless heap, lying on top of one another. No one moved, twitched, or made a sound; four of the street fighters were out for the count. By this time the fifth one was shaking and trembling violently from head to toe, swaying around like a tightrope walker about to lose his balance, desperately trying to avoid falling on his colleagues. Somehow he remained upright.

This seemed the appropriate time to make my exit. "I'm off now," I said.

"What …" Derek began. "What shall I do when they come round?" he asked, looking helpless.

"Acts nine," I replied, grabbed my coat, and went.

So that's what he did—he read to them about Paul falling on the floor as a persecutor of Christians and rising as a preacher of the gospel. They were fascinated, came back again and again, and one day they turned up at my place, with Derek, for a meeting in our church. The two words, "Let's ask God to come" and "You're not chicken, are you?" with the subsequent signs and wonders, certainly helped us preach the gospel to them. Sometimes a word or two from the Holy Spirit can help us proclaim the kingdom.

God's Timing

Back in Bible days evangelistic activity took place whenever God directed the traffic, regularly leading people to the right place at the right time in order to hear the good news of Jesus.

In Acts 8, Philip is having a good time preaching in Samaria, where many are being saved, healed, and delivered. Suddenly God speaks to him, first by an angel and then by the Spirit, telling him to leave Samaria and go to an Ethiopian official. It is an unexpected call and not one Philip could have discerned naturally. No one minds being called somewhere else when things are going badly, or not going at all, but when "all paid close attention to what he said" and "evil spirits came out of many, and many paralytics and cripples were healed" (Acts 8:6–7), it is surprising that God should decide to redeploy him. But the timing, of course, being God's timing,

was perfect. When Philip reaches the Ethiopian, he is already reading Isaiah 53 and is ripe to hear the gospel, to which he responds
and Philip baptizes him in water. It must rate as one of the easiest
instances of evangelism ever.

My friend Bill's conversion was a little more complicated. We
not only needed a word from God, but thirty years of waiting. Once
more it was God's timing and a word from the Spirit that helped
the process. Like so many others, Bill thought church would be dull
and irrelevant, so he never came. His wife, Margaret, was a committed Christian member of our congregation who prayed regularly for
thirty years for her husband's conversion, but with no success. While
Margaret went to church, Bill stayed at home.

One day Bill became ill and went to the hospital for major surgery. I visited him; he was pleased to see me and very grateful for
the prayers, especially those said for him in church, which Margaret
told him about. It didn't seem right to lay hands on him or pray in
his presence at the time, so I assured Bill of our love, support, and
prayers. As well as praying for him in meetings, quite a few others
prayed regularly for him in private. In due course Bill made a normal
recovery following his operation, but came home only to discover
that his business had gone rapidly downhill, and he was now bank-
rupt. Unemployment, with its loss of dignity and sense of failure, left
him very empty, so when Margaret nagged Bill for the umpteenth
time to come to church, he came. Good timing—God's timing—is
often so important when it comes to evangelism.

Evensong was not Bill's scene and he looked very uncomfortable with it. He was obviously not a regular churchgoer because he
chose a seat right down front and then found he couldn't see when

everybody else chose to stand, sit down, or kneel. He tried to be good, kept looking round to check he was adopting the right posture, but about the only thing he heard was my announcement about a time of ministry following the service. We chatted briefly when the evening service ended.

"Thank you for visiting me, Peter, and praying," he said. "As you can see, I'm fine now."

"No problem, Bill," I replied. "A pleasure."

"I thought I'd come to say thank you," he continued. "But I'm afraid I couldn't get on with that evensong. Not my cup of tea, I'm afraid."

"Never mind, Bill," I said. "Come again at Christmas and sing a few carols."

"Right," he said. "I'll do that." And then he paused while I waited. "But what's this ministry?" he asked. "What happens then?"

I was slightly embarrassed and struggling to find the right response when suddenly three words of Scripture rose from deep within me, came into my mind, and popped out. "Come and see," I said, recalling John 1:46.

"All right," he said. "I will."

Out of curiosity, he joined us in the side-chapel. From what happened subsequently, I believe this occurrence was another word of wisdom from the Holy Spirit. It opened the door to everything and everyone for Bill—especially to the Spirit.

There were about fifteen people present when I asked the Holy Spirit to come and minister to us. Never having experienced anything like this before, Bill didn't know what to expect, but he saw others standing, eyes closed, hands held out, and did the same. Slowly he became hot and began to perspire as his hands started shaking from side to side. This puzzled Bill at first and he tried to stop it, but when he found he couldn't control the shaking, he relaxed into this new experience until eventually the sensation began to leave him. Afterward we were talking again.

"What was that?" he asked, imitating what had happened to him with a shake of both hands.

"That was Jesus," I explained.

"Do you do this every week?" he asked.

"Yes," I said, "and you'll be most welcome any time."

"I didn't like the first service much," he said apologetically, "but I'll have some more of that," and shook his hands once more to make sure I understood what he was after.

Bill came again, to the later session, and this time he knew what to expect. He stood quickly after my invitation, closed his eyes, held his hands out, and after I invoked the Holy Spirit, began shaking almost immediately. This time it didn't faze him one iota—this was why he'd come; it was what he was expecting. He wasn't, however, expecting what happened next. As yet more power came upon him, he crashed to the floor and slid under a television that we had on a table in the side-chapel. It was covered with a blue cloth, and Bill's disappearance underneath it was somewhat reminiscent of a coffin's departure through the curtains at a crematorium. He was there one moment and gone the next.

The rest of us carried on as normal, until after about a quarter of an hour we heard a noise that sounded like someone knocking on the door or trying to get up from under a table and banging his head. We all looked toward the table, saw the curtains part, and watched as a man in his fifties crawled out on all fours, rubbing his bald patch.

People helped Bill to his feet and he staggered about like a drunkard until finally, held up by two strong supporters, he looked straight at me and asked, "Was that Jesus too?" This time Bill needed nothing more elaborate than a nod of my head to confirm his suspicions.

Throughout it all, despite the powerful and (to some) disturbing activity, Bill displayed a countenance that positively glowed like the morning sun. What happened to him would not have suited everyone, but it definitely suited Bill. And yet, according to his own testimony, an even bigger turning point came the night a young married man fell onto the floor, face down.

As the man lay on the floor, demons began tormenting him, causing him to shout out. I offered to take him apart privately, but he said, "No. Do it here. I don't mind. I just want to be rid of them."

So Bill and the others watched me confront these demons publicly, like Jesus did. I commanded the demons in Jesus' name to reveal their identities and to come out. Eventually three appeared to depart, one at a time, through the mouth. All who were there could see the manifestations of the demons as they left, and the change on the young man's face as God's peace replaced Satan's stress. Bill was amazed and kept nudging his neighbor throughout to make sure he was seeing it too.

From then on Bill was born again by the Spirit. He read the Bible, attended Bible classes, spoke in tongues, became confirmed in the church, and went on to lead Bible studies, prayer times, and ministry sessions in his own home. He also came regularly to church on Sunday evenings, sang in the robed choir, and learned to enjoy evensong. One day he came out of church to find that his car had been stolen. "Praise the Lord it was mine and not someone else's," he said. "I'd have hated anyone not to come back because of this."

I find it interesting that Bill did not continue to shake or fall under the Spirit's power; it seems that in Bill's case, this kind of power came on him specifically as part of his conversion experience, as with Paul (Acts 9:1–19).

Bill accepted Jesus Christ as his Lord and Savior after experiencing physical healing, the power of the Holy Spirit in his body, power over demons, and the Word of God explaining it all to him. These were proclamations of the kingdom of God in word, deed, sign, and power that encouraged Bill to be born again of the Spirit. His salvation came from responding to the Word of God in faith—but it was the deeds, signs, and demonstrations of power that opened Bill up to the Word and gave him the faith to accept Jesus. This was God's timing for Bill, and a word of wisdom from the Holy Spirit helped set it up. I recently heard Bill share his story, now over twenty years since his conversion, and the moment when I used the words "come and see" featured prominently in his own account.

God's Presence

When we become Christians, we receive the Holy Spirit permanently inside us (Rom. 8:9). This is the presence of God. The activity of the Holy Spirit then comes and goes as He chooses (Heb. 2:4). This means that we do not have spiritual gifts in our pockets or handbags that we can take out whenever we feel like it; what we have is the gift of the Holy Spirit.

Paul's list of nine spiritual gifts in 1 Corinthians 12 is merely a categorization or clarification so that we are not ignorant of the things God might want to do (1 Cor. 12:1). When Jesus proclaimed the kingdom of God, He wasn't working His way through a list or deciding which gifts to use; rather, the Spirit provided whatever He needed. Take a look at Jesus using these spiritual gifts:

Words of knowledge	(John 1:47–48; 4:16–18)
Miracles	(John 2:11; 6:14)
Healing	(John 5:8–9; 9:6–7)
Wisdom	(John 8:7; Matt. 22:18–22)
Distinguishing between spirits	(Mark 9:25; Luke 13:16)
Prophecy	(Matt. 24—25; John 13:38)
Faith	(John 11:43–44; 19:30)

Can you think of the two that are missing? Most of these, if not all of them, helped Jesus proclaim the kingdom. The disciples in the early church did something similar.

When Peter and John saw a man by the temple gate who was crippled, they didn't work through a list to see if they had the gifts or not. The Spirit of Jesus gave them what they needed, the man was healed, and many more people believed (Acts 3:1–10; 4:4). The disciples then spread the good news making use of the spiritual gifts God gave them.

Words of knowledge	(Acts 4; 10; 11)
Miracles	(Acts 9:40–42)
Healing	(Acts 3:1–10)
Wisdom	(Acts 16:28–40)
Distinguishing between spirits	(Acts 16:16–18)
Prophecy	(Acts 11:27–30; 21:10–11)
Faith	(Acts 14:8–10)
Interpretation of tongues	(Acts 2:5–11)
Speaking in tongues	(Acts 2:3–4)

In Acts there are references to all nine of the spiritual gifts, including healing, helping the followers to proclaim the kingdom of God. As Paul says, "All these are the work of one and the same Spirit, and he gives them to each one, just as he determines" (1 Cor. 12:11).

David was my colleague at Canford Magna before he retired and kindly wrote this account describing when God spoke through him supernaturally, using a spiritual gift, just as on the day of Pentecost.

The first occasion I spoke in tongues was at a renewal meeting at the City Temple in London where Jean Stone was speaking. She talked about the bumper bundle of spiritual blessings, which is the birthright of every Christian, and in particular about the more supernatural gifts of the Spirit, including speaking in tongues—a wonderful prayer language of praise and prayer.

At the end of the meeting she invited all those wanting to receive this gift to come to the front. I wanted everything she had described so I was up there like a shot. "How did you become a Christian in the first place?" she asked. "By believing God's promise and asking in faith. And it's just the same principle for receiving any gift from God—believe, ask, and receive." So I asked for tongues, believed God would give it, opened my mouth, and a beautiful language I'd never learned began to tumble from my lips. I felt it begin to flow, and knew I was expressing praise and worship to God with an exhilarating freedom and joy. That was over forty-five years ago now, and ever since then I've used this precious gift and valued it enormously.

My prayer language sounded Slavic or Russian, and there have been a number of times down the years when people have recognized it. The first was at a prayer meeting in our house when I was a theological student. During the meeting I prayed out loud in tongues, and afterward my college tutor who was there said he'd been a Russian interpreter in the Royal Air Force during national service, and although I wasn't speaking Russian itself, it was something similar, and he recognized a number of words of Slavic origin including those for "prayer," "God," and "Jesus." Although I didn't need reassurance about it, I was greatly encouraged that this was a definite language.

Similar comments came at other times—after several years a clergy colleague who had been a language teacher recognized it as a Slavic language, and on another occasion many years later when I was praying in tongues for two university students in Nottingham, one of them burst out, "I'm learning Russian, and I can understand you—you're praising God and saying how great He is."

I had a vivid experience of the reality and powerful influence of tongues during my time as a vicar in Kent. Our phone rang, and a man speaking with a broken English accent asked if I was a Protestant pastor, because he needed to talk to one. I said I was and drove to meet him in the local supermarket car park from where he'd rung. He got in the car and we talked together for a long time.

It was a hard-luck story, but with intriguing elements. He told me his family had come to England at the end of the Second World War as refugees from Eastern Europe. He was a young boy at the time. He'd been through many ups and downs over the subsequent forty years, but the gist of his story was that he was now at the end of his rope and needed help. Alongside his obvious practical hardship, he was searching for spiritual help as well. He felt ashamed to ask God, but was so desperate he'd found my name in the phone book and rung me up.

I felt that familiar nudge from the Holy Spirit, and at the end of our conversation I suggested we should pray. I led him through some honest prayers expressing his needs, asking for God's forgiveness, and inviting Jesus to help him out in a life-changing way. I didn't tell him I was going to, but I then prayed for him in tongues.

Afterward I asked him how he felt about our prayer time. He said to me, "That was amazing. When I was a boy early in the war, our village was overrun and occupied by the Russian army. There was a big army hospital nearby, and we had two Russian soldiers billeted in our house for the rest of the war, and got to know them well. They talked together in their own language, and over the years they taught me to understand quite a lot of it. You were speaking in their language. You kept talking about green fields and bunches of grapes. And you used a word which I don't know in English, but it was the title given to these soldiers to describe their work in the hospital. Their job was to help patients out of bed and support them as they walked down the wards."

"In the Bible bunches of grapes and green fields are used as a picture of God's blessing and provision," I said to him, "and the word you're looking for but don't know in English is 'Comforter.' It's a biblical name for the Holy Spirit—the Paraclete—literally 'the one who comes alongside to help.' I believe God is saying that He knows your needs, has heard your prayers, and that the Holy Spirit is going to help you out." He was incredibly moved, and very grateful—and I was so thrilled that God had spoken to him so clearly—through this unusual use of the gift of tongues.

When the Holy Spirit comes upon us he helps us to proclaim the kingdom—sometimes in our own language and sometimes supernaturally.

The Right Time and Place

If we are to be fishers of men, we need to fish at the right time, in the right place, and put the net on the right side of the boat (Luke 5:1–11). In Mark 1:21–34, Jesus receives an amazing response to His first sermon in Capernaum, but the following morning while it is still dark, He slips away alone to pray (Mark 1:35–39). Most of us know how much we need to pray before ministry, but Jesus knew how much He needed to pray *after* ministry. Simon and his companions seek Him out and enthuse about the ministry in Capernaum, but Jesus replies, "Let us go somewhere else" (Mark 1:38). A few days later Jesus returns to Capernaum (Mark 2:1). As Jesus only did what He saw the Father doing, I think we can assume that through His prayer relationship, the Holy Spirit told Jesus where and when to proclaim the kingdom.

These sort of directions also shape Paul's missionary journeys:

> While they were worshiping the Lord and fasting, the
> Holy Spirit said, "Set apart for me Barnabas and Saul
> for the work to which I have called them." So after

> they had fasted and prayed, they placed their hands
> on them and sent them off. The two of them, sent on
> their way by the Holy Spirit, went down to Seleucia
> and sailed from there to Cyprus. (Acts 13:2–4)

God calls Paul and Barnabas to go and proclaim the kingdom, and by His Holy Spirit directs them to Seleucia and Cyprus. In Acts 16:6, Paul is "kept by the Holy Spirit from preaching the word in the province of Asia" and also Bithynia (verse 7), but in verse 9, he receives a vision telling him to go to Macedonia. In Acts 22:17–18, Paul recalls how earlier, while praying, he fell into a trance and was told to leave Jerusalem, but in Acts 20:22–23, he is "compelled by the Spirit" to return to Jerusalem. Finally, in Acts 27:24, an angel tells him he will arrive safely in Rome. Hearing the Spirit speak not only helps us proclaim the kingdom at the right time, it can direct us to the right place, too.

A man who lived on the outskirts of Birmingham became exceedingly depressed as a result of a series of traumas. Times were hard, he lost his job, and his wife left him and took the kids. Darkness spread all around and within him, and he decided to end it all. As a last throw of the dice, he cried out to God.

A friend of mine was praying one day when he sensed the Holy Spirit moving on him in power, through heat and shaking, and strange words formed in his head. "Go into town, to the Bullring (the shopping center), and ask the first man you see if he would like to find God."

In desperation the depressed man yelled out to God: "I'm going into town. If a man does not approach me in the Bullring and ask me if I would like to find God, I shall end my life there and then."

My friend was not very keen on going into the Birmingham city center that day. He had no car and very little money, and wasting what he did have on two bus journeys chasing wild geese did not seem a very good idea at the time. But the feeling grew stronger and the Holy Spirit persisted, so without telling anyone else, lest they think him a fool, he went—in his own eyes as a fool for Christ.

When he came through the tunnel into the Bullring market, a man was walking straight toward him looking downcast but determined, as if he had some evil intent in mind.

"Excuse me, sir," asked my friend. "But would you like to find God?"

The rest, as they say, is history. The man did find God, or perhaps it was God who found him; he did not commit suicide and, of course, because God initiated the encounter, the timing and the place were perfect. To God be all the glory!

Jesus said to a Samaritan woman, "You have had five husbands, and the man you now have is not your husband" (John 4:18). As a result she believed in Jesus, fetched many more from the village to hear him, and they became believers too.

It may also be that Jesus had a word from God about the name and whereabouts of Zacchaeus when he was in the sycamore-fig tree. Certainly Jesus sought, found, and saved the lost that day with very little human effort (Luke 19:9–10).

A word of knowledge from the Holy Spirit may come as a piece of information about somebody, something, or some event supernaturally given by the Father (1 Cor. 12:8). It acts as a trigger that arouses interest, encourages belief, and leads to the proclamation of the King and the kingdom. In the example of Zacchaeus, the pieces of information are in themselves small and unspectacular: a man in a fig tree in a hot land full of fig trees and knowledge of his name. No cynic would have been convinced by these particular words, but the Spirit gives them to those who are seeking and ready to receive God's word.

On the other hand, the word given to the Samaritan woman contained significant details about the woman's personal life that Jesus was unlikely to know naturally, and this word helped her to respond in faith to Jesus.

Spectacular or not, all of these words came from the Spirit to help Jesus do what the Father was doing, and because the same Holy Spirit is present in believers today, we can do likewise. Through hearing the Spirit speak, we receive signs to arouse interest and to build up faith in people, preparing them to receive the good news.

The Five-Year Plan

Narrator: Then the eleven disciples went to Galilee, to the mountain, where Jesus told them to go. Jesus came to them and said, "Go into all the world and preach the good news to all creation!" Then he left them and was taken in to heaven (see Mark 16:15–19).

John: Just can't imagine it. Go into all the world. What on? What with? No details. No money. No modern technology. We haven't got much going for us.

Peter: Surely if Jesus had intended us to do a sales pitch on this—to sell the unsellable—he'd have given us more details. Maps. Plans. Target groups. Budgets. Office staff

and equipment. Advertising agencies. Management structures. Premises. Transport. You name it. We haven't got it.

John: You don't think we'll turn the world upside down
then?

Peter: To plan something like this, we'd have to bring
the skills of big business in. Not enough brains among us.

John: You're right. We need some academics. University
trained. Languages, theology, philosophy. Someone who
could write it impressively, with long words.

Peter: What about a five-year plan? If we are to go into
the world and preach the good news to all creation, I think
we need a plan.

Pause.

John: He didn't say anything about a plan did He? "Just
go to Jerusalem and wait," He said.

Peter: OK, that's it then. No five-year plan. We go into
Jerusalem and wait.

In 1993 we moved from inner-city Birmingham to the Elysian fields
of Dorset where I inherited the eccentric son of an archdeacon as my
youth worker. Johnny had gained credence in the eyes of the local
youth by furnishing his house with items from the local dump and
letting anybody and everybody know they were welcome at all hours.
He made no five-year plan, but he did do a lot of prayer.

On one occasion three lads, who were into hard-core music and
had attended Johnny's "rave" style meetings, dropped in and drank

coffee in his kitchen. Welcoming them was one thing, but getting rid of them proved to be quite another, and it was only long after the youths had outstayed their welcome that the Holy Spirit gave the legal tenant an idea to move them on.

"You'll have to go now," said Johnny. "I'm about to have my quiet time."

"What's that?" inquired the three musketeers.

"It's when I speak to God and He speaks to me," replied our youth leader. The inquirers tried to control themselves but failed. They fell about laughing, then one of them cursed badly, but Johnny kept going, realizing his approach was maybe helping his visitors on their way.

"God's here right now," he said. There was a moment's pause and then more laughter. "Will you say one for me?" the visitors asked in turn, sounding lighthearted and cynical, but Johnny's answer was serious.

"Yes," he said, "on one condition. I'll say one for each of you providing you are prepared for God to speak back to you." They agreed and left. Johnny was pleased to see them go, having been made something of a laughingstock, but what he did not know was that his three friends had concealed an encounter they all experienced.

As they left, one of them said to the others, "Did you feel that? When he said, 'God's here right now,' something nearly pushed me over. I had to hang onto the kitchen unit to stop myself falling on the floor."

All three felt the power of God but refused to let Johnny see what was happening to them. In the quiet time that followed, Johnny asked for a word for each of them.

"Lord," he prayed. "What would you like to say to Lee?" The Spirit of God spoke to him with impressions in his mind, and Johnny wrote them all down. He did the same for Matt and Jo.

After the next meeting Johnny gave the three of them a lift home in his van, and when they stopped at Lee's place, Johnny handed him an envelope. "This is for you, Lee," he said, "from the Lord." As he handed it to him, power came upon the two sitting in the back and they both began to shake.

Lee took the envelope, walked away, then came back and knocked at the window. "What happens if He talks to me?" he asked with some trepidation as he recognized this might be a bigger force than he'd met before. Johnny reassured him and gave advice about the God of love who could be invited to come into his life through Jesus, or be kept out by saying no.

At home Lee opened the envelope and read the words. *How did he know?* he kept asking himself. *How did he know what my life is like, what I'm thinking, and what I'm feeling?* He went to speak to his parents, who themselves were in the process of becoming Jehovah's Witnesses, and Lee asked them if they minded him becoming a Christian. They gave their son permission; Lee asked the Lord Jesus Christ to come into his life to save him, and as he did so peace and power entered in.

Meanwhile the other two were still shaking in the back of the van. "Got one for me?" they both asked in a wobbly kind of way. Incredible power kept going through them until four in the morning, and the only way they could describe it was like being high on speed without aftereffects.

The words on both pieces of paper were as accurate as the ones Lee received and spoke right into the heart of their differing situations. Matt couldn't cope. He ripped up the paper, flushed it away, and went home—but failed to get much sleep. He moved from being agnostic to believing in God but he did not, at the time, make a commitment to Jesus Christ.

Jo, on the other hand, started coming to our Lantern Church, had regular chats with Johnny and others, and eventually went forward to ask for prayer. This began a real move of God's Holy Spirit among the young people's group, which at one point reached 180 members.

Like Peter and John, Johnny waited on God, and God came.

5

HEALING THE EMOTIONS

At the end of the evening service I invited everybody to stand, close their eyes, hold out their hands, and welcome God the Father, through Jesus, to send His Holy Spirit upon us to do whatever He wanted to do. There was an expectancy—people were hoping, believing, trusting—having worshipped God and praised Him for over an hour. There were probably about forty people there; we asked Him to come, and He came.

Instantly I could sense things happening with a significant number of people. The Spirit touched some; others waited on Him and spent time with God in a busy world, and the Lord gave me a few words that were confirmed afterward. God was in this place.

After a while I released the ministry teams to go to individuals as they felt led, and subsequently I gave everyone the opportunity to ask for specific prayer for themselves or for others, especially those not well enough to be present. Suddenly, just as I was about to say a closing prayer, there was a scene—a big one.

A strong lady, whom I knew reasonably well and who regularly came to some of our sessions from another church, started screaming and yelling, disturbing the whole place. Ministry team members rushed to help, and those who arrived first were powerfully thumped. Some of our experienced people had a go at helping, but with the shrieking and hitting still going on, they came to get me.

Observing the fracas I made the decision not to get too close, as I am the one who leads services, and a black eye or a few teeth knocked out doesn't look very good. Instead I chose to stand about ten feet away and allowed the laity to remain nearer. I stood there for a while listening to the noise, watching the violence. Eventually I spoke.

"Margaret, do you know what is happening?" I asked from a distance.

"Yes," she said, in a panic.

"What is happening?" I asked firmly.

"My older brother and two of his friends are molesting me in the garden shed," she said forcefully. (It turned out they were about twelve or thirteen years old in her mind.)

Jesus wants to bring peace and love, but sometimes the Holy Spirit allows our emotional pain to surface so we can identify it—a step on the way to healing. But this can generate a bit of a mess. Fortunately some of the people in this church were familiar with such scenes but, even so, everybody was disturbed; nobody liked what was happening, and the situation needed to be resolved.

"Can you see Jesus?" I asked Margaret.

"No," she replied hysterically.

"Holy Spirit, please help Margaret to see Jesus," I prayed.

At moments like these, I make sure I do not picture what I think ought to happen. I do not visualize Jesus by Galilee, taking the children on His knee or feeding the hungry. I do not think about Jesus dying on the cross, rising from the tomb, or ascending into heaven. What I do is to ask the Father, through Jesus, to send His Holy Spirit to Margaret so that she can see Jesus, and He can choose whatever He wants to do. He can create any visions or pictures; He can bring any images He needs into the situation to bring healing or anything else He wants to do, because He is God.

"Oh," she said, taken by surprise. "Jesus has just come into the garden shed. He is brushing off my brother and his two friends and throwing them out."

At this point Margaret stopped thrashing around. In her mind's eye she saw Jesus turn away from her while she adjusted her clothing, and then He threw open the door so that she could come out into the garden and the fresh air. Within seconds she still looked disturbed, worried, and afraid, but the yelling ceased. She then described to us how Jesus took her into the garden for a walk.

Jesus said, "I love you. Come and see how much I care for you." They then talked among the trees, the flowers, and the birds, under a lemon sun and a sapphire sky.

Being the kind of person who does not keep things to herself, Margaret then described her spiritual encounter with Jesus as she talked to Him naturally, albeit emotionally, and we witnessed her countenance glow in the presence of the Holy Spirit.

Margaret knew it was Jesus. She was a born-again Christian, and the Spirit was able to "take from what belonged to Jesus'" and make it known to her (see John 16:15). With the help of her Lord she forgave her brother and his friends, and began to face up to the whole incident. The ministry was costly in terms of time, bruises, and embarrassment, but we were pleased for Margaret for her own sake, and for the privilege of serving Jesus.

When it was all over, we committed Margaret into God's hands, prayed for Jesus to go on healing her, and she went home on the bus. Margaret sat upstairs on the top of a double-decker bus and looked out of the window, but she said afterward, "I was actually much higher than that. I wasn't just on the top of the bus; I was floating in a bubble with Jesus." After reflecting for a week or two, Margaret realized all her relationships with men had gone wrong from the age of ten, probably stemming from this incident.

Margaret continued to spend time with Jesus, sometimes dwelling in the past, and sometimes in the present, as she regularly asked the Holy Spirit to come to her daily, as we taught her to do, and eventually she felt sufficiently healed to move on.

Jesus and Emotional Healing

Most Christians believe that Jesus healed people physically, but we see in the Gospels that He also brought emotional wholeness to people. There were several He helped in this way, preparing them for the work God wanted them to do.

The advantage of Jesus as the model to follow, even in the realm of emotional wholeness, is that He is perfect.

> For we do not have a high priest who is unable to sympathize with our weaknesses, but we have one who has been tempted in every way, just as we are—yet was without sin. (Heb. 4:15)

Jesus was a man who acknowledged and expressed His feelings. "When he saw the crowds, he had compassion on them, because they were harassed and helpless, like sheep without a shepherd" (Matt. 9:36). Jesus was grieved when John the Baptist was beheaded. "He withdrew by boat privately to a solitary place" (Matt. 14:13). When the seventy-two cast out demons in his name, Jesus was "full of joy" (Luke 10:21). At the death of Lazarus, "Jesus wept" (John 11:35). Again, "as he approached Jerusalem and saw the city, he wept over it" (Luke 19:41).

Jesus was bereaved, He was sad, and He wept at the fate of Jerusalem. When the disciples rejoiced, He was full of joy—and all of that was okay. Good emotions. Helpful feelings. In touch with reality. Being angry at the hypocrisy of the Pharisees and the misuse of the temple was okay too. Anger at sin is allowed. To those who sold doves He said, "Get these out of here! How dare you turn my Father's house into a market!" (John 2:16).

The Gospels describe Jesus—who was fully human—experiencing right emotions, in the right places. And then we encounter Him in the garden of Gethsemane. Here is something of a problem. What happens doesn't seem to fit our normal view of Jesus as the perfect man. It is worth looking at.

We are able to eavesdrop on Jesus because it all happened in the presence of a witness. "A young man, wearing nothing but a linen garment, was following Jesus" (Mark 14:51). Many think this is the painter's signature, so to speak—certainly it is not found in the other Gospels. Could this be Mark himself, following, watching, listening, remembering, providing an authentic eyewitness account of the problematical incident?

With my writer's hat on, I'd say that in the context of the Gospels the story of Jesus in Gethsemane makes no sense at all. But with my counselor's hat on, knowing the importance of dealing with our emotions, this account makes total sense.

The Problem

Seven times Jesus has warned His disciples that He has come to Jerusalem to die. In the last warning—the Last Supper—Jesus uses bread for His body and red wine for His blood to graphically demonstrate that He won't be eating and drinking with them again until after the resurrection. This is definitely the Last Supper—when Jesus prophesies things that are to happen—and then seems to change His mind.

A few minutes later, in the garden of Gethsemane on the lower slopes of the Mount of Olives, Jesus is deeply distressed and troubled, overwhelmed with sorrow to the point of death. Jesus prays, "*Abba,* Father … everything is possible for you. Take this cup from me" (Mark 14:36).

The Messiah has come—the Son of God, anointed by the Spirit with signs and wonders galore. Moses and Elijah appeared at the transfiguration to strengthen Him for what was to come in Jerusalem. Seven times after that Jesus predicted His death, the last time only a few moments before Gethsemane. Now He seems to pray, "I'm a celebrity. Get me out of here."

The Solution

Until the Last Supper, Jesus kept Himself alive against all the odds in order to teach and prepare His disciples and, to a lesser extent, His other followers. His goal was to accomplish two tasks:

Task 1: To stay alive until the Passover Feast so that the whole world could understand the sacrifice—with visual aids of bread and wine—telling us why He died.

Task 2: To stop the disciples from being killed in battle, or committing suicide after His death and before He rose again.

Jesus has given everything to prepare the world, and in particular the apostles, so that they may know they need a Savior. Now that all the plans are made, Jesus has a few moments to Himself—with His Father—before the soldiers come to arrest Him. This is time to confront His own feelings so that He can walk through the next twenty-four hours emotionally prepared. And how privileged we are to experience it.

Having cared for and prepared others, having been totally obedient to the Father and done everything asked of Him, He now allows the emotional pain buried deep inside to come to the surface. This is the supreme example of emotional health—modeled for us at the tensest moment in human history. Jesus will need to be emotionally whole if He is to face the arrest, trial, flogging, and crucifixion, and still pray, "Father, forgive them, for they do not know what they are doing" (Luke 23:34). So He expresses His feelings out loud to God (and for Mark to hear): "Father … take this cup from me" (Mark 14:36).

The key to understanding the incident in Gethsemane is this: *Emotions are neutral.*

What we feel is what we feel. Truth is truth. Sin—or lack of sin—is what we choose to do with what we feel. It's not what we feel.

So—if Jesus is sad, happy, or angry—they are His emotions, and acknowledging how He is feeling helps Jesus, like any other human being, to make the right responses to His situation.

There is no sin in emotions, and no sin in expressing them out loud to God. How I feel is how I feel. It is truth. I'm hurting. I don't want this. I'm not praying out loud for the benefit of others—but for me. This is hell and I'm not enjoying it.

Jesus did it again on the cross, this time quoting Psalm 22: "My God, my God, why have you forsaken me?" (Mark 15:34)—a reminder that the laments of the Psalms are also part of the Word of God. They cry out to Him, share pain, express emotions, and tell it the way it is. By externalizing His emotional thoughts, Jesus clarifies the situation and receives the help He needs from His Father. He is expressing total dependency, so characteristic of the Son of Man in the Gospels, displaying His trust in His Father.

Jesus is not changing His mind—He is checking that the Father has not changed His. Once He knows what His feelings are, but also what God the Father feels, there is total obedience. Jesus has brought His emotions to the surface, making sure everything is in order to serve the Father totally: in spirit, body, mind, will, and emotions. In Gethsemane and on the cross, Jesus demonstrates to the world how to get in touch with emotions as He prepares to face the agony without sin and accomplish the Father's will.

A Word of Lament

As a theology student I had to do hospital visits on Sunday mornings. I'd never done this before, and as I arrived at the ward for the first time, the sister grabbed me. "See what you can do for the situation in the far bed on the left," she said. "Suicide attempt." None of the nurses wanted to bother with this patient—they wanted to nurse those who wanted to live—so I was dispatched.

I hesitated. "Go on," she said. "Last bed on the left." She was a formidable sister, so I made my first ever hospital visit to the most difficult person in the ward. Fortunately, like Jesus in the garden of Gethsemane, I had been prepared. At college I attended lectures by Dr. Frank Lake—the Christian psychiatrist—who taught us the importance of Psalm 88. He loved to get us to say it together at the start of a lecture, as an act of worship. Let me give you a taste.

> My soul is full of trouble and my life draws near the
>   grave....
>   I am like a man without strength.
> I am set apart with the dead,
>   like the slain who lie in the grave....
>   My eyes are dim with grief....
> From my youth I have been afflicted and close to
>   death;
>   I have suffered your terrors and am in despair....
> You have taken my companions and loved ones from
>   me;
>   the darkness is my closest friend.

At the end Frank would say: "Glory be to the Father and to the Son and to the Spirit. As it was in the beginning, so it is now and ever shall be. Amen."

The Holy Spirit inspired the laments in the Psalms for our good. So shout at God—tell it the way it is—as Jesus did in Gethsemane and on the cross.

"Tell me about it," I said to the lady who had tried to take her own life, and I didn't have to speak again for half an hour as the young person in the hospital bed poured it all out to me. She was in her twenties, as I was at the time, and moaned and groaned about her life and her circumstances, repeating that there was no point in living anymore.

I began to know how the nurses felt as her depression and darkness enveloped me as well. And then she finished, with these questions:

"So—you're religious then? You believe in God? Why should I go on living?"

Other students appeared at this moment at the end of the ward indicating that it was time to go or we'd miss Sunday lunch. I looked around for help. There on the bedside table was a Gideon's Bible, and I grabbed it as a security blanket. "What you need to do," I said, sounding more confident than I felt, "is to read Psalm 88. If you're here next week, I'll see you again then. Psalm 88." And then I left.

On the following Sunday she was still there, beside the same bed. I chatted with a few others first to prepare myself for the ordeal, and then eventually I moved on to the "suicide attempt" in the corner. When I arrived, I was amazed to see the lady fully dressed in a chair with no drip, face beaming. She grabbed my hand.

"Thank you," she said. "Thank you. I never knew. I never knew before—I'm in the Bible. Psalm 88. Every word fitted me—it was as if every word was written by God for me. I'm all right now. Going home soon. I want to live again—somebody else knows how I feel. That's all I needed. God must have sent you."

The Community of Faith

Jesus said to His disciples, "I have much more to say to you, more than you can now bear" (John 16:12). After His resurrection, but before the Feast of Pentecost, Jesus set about bringing healing to the community of faith. They now needed to be restored and prepared for the anointing of the Holy Spirit so that they could hear God's voice and receive power to take the gospel of Jesus Christ into the world.

Only now were they able to understand, receive healing, and be put right with God, one another, and themselves. There was much work to be done, however. Here are five examples:

Mary

Jesus began preparing His mother at the cross.

> When Jesus saw his mother there, and the disciple whom he loved standing nearby, he said to his mother, "Dear woman, here is your son," and to the disciple, "Here is your mother." From that time on, the disciple took her into his home. (John 19:26–27)

Jesus' family had said, "He is out of his mind" (Mark 3:21). So from the cross Jesus exercised His authority as the eldest to move His mother from a household of unbelievers to the community of faith. Whatever else this achieved, it brought considerable healing to His mother to be with John in the Easter weekend when John found the empty tomb and believed (John 20:8).

James

Then Jesus turned His attention to the one who had become the head of the family. "Then he appeared to James," His brother (1 Cor. 15:7). James and Jude, two of Jesus' brothers, wrote epistles in the New Testament, and Paul recorded Jesus' visit to James as something of significance. It looks as if Jesus' visit to His brother enabled him to believe and be restored, because he became the chairman of the council of Jerusalem (Acts 15:13–21).

Cleopas

Tradition has it that Cleopas was the brother of Joseph, making him Jesus' uncle, and some think that he may have been with his wife on the road to Emmaus. Jesus appeared to them in a form that was not immediately recognizable. He seemingly appeared from nowhere and later disappeared from their sight. They later described this spiritual encounter with Jesus as "our hearts burning within us" (Luke 24:32). The experienced changed them.

Mary Magdalene

The incident with the emotional Mary Magdalene on Easter morning was similar. Mary did not recognize Jesus immediately, but He changed her (John 20:11–18).

Judas Iscariot

The opportunity for restoration, however, that most people miss is what Jesus put in place for Judas. During the course of the Passover, a child would have normally asked, as part of the liturgy, "Why is this night different from all other nights?" During the Last

Supper, this tradition may have given rise to the disciples' discussion about which of them was the greatest. They wanted to determine which of them was the least and therefore most suited to play the role of the child. The leader of the Passover liturgy dips the sop and, even today, gives it to the person whom he loves the most, normally his wife. "Then, dipping the piece of bread, [Jesus] gave it to Judas Iscariot, son of Simon" (John 13:26). It looks as if Jesus also wanted to save and heal and restore Judas, if he was willing.

Jesus loved Mary and Judas; He had personal encounters with Mary Magdalene and Cleopas; He visited James, the disciples, and Peter. In every case, except that of Judas, Jesus' words, love, and spiritual presence positively changed those whom He met and healed them emotionally.

Ministering to Those Who Have Been Badly Hurt

Whenever we ask the Holy Spirit to come to do whatever He wants to do, we run the risk that God will bring to the surface that which is hidden in darkness, as happened with Margaret remembering her abuse. If it is an isolated incident, asking the Holy Spirit to bring healing often resolves the situation, particularly when the person is able to forgive those who have hurt them. "For if you forgive men when they sin against you, your heavenly Father will also forgive you" (Matt. 6:14).

But for those who have suffered a lifetime of abuse, this is sometimes not sufficient, and it is often very difficult for ordinary church ministry teams to cope in terms of time and expertise. Sometimes all we can do is allow the Holy Spirit to show us there is a problem so that more experienced professionals can address the situation. Knowing when we are out of our depth is very important for Christians who try to help, even for ministry teams containing accredited counselors.

Christian doctors, psychiatrists, and psychologists in our congregations have offered great assistance to me in my ministry. Even so, the biblical principles we find in stories like the healing of Thomas (see below) can help us all.

Jesus helps us turn and face the pain of our emotional problems. On one occasion a friend needed the help of psychiatrists and was admitted into the hospital and put on drugs, but eventually the medical staff recommended electroconvulsive therapy (ECT). We were not keen, so my friend carried out her own research among a number of patients in the ward. She discovered that many people felt better initially, for about four or five weeks, after which they felt worse. The treatment seemed to bring about no permanent solution.

The staff of the hospital, including the chief psychiatrist, other doctors, a Christian psychologist, and the nurses helping in the case all discussed my friend. The Christian psychologist reported their conclusions to me. Apparently the chief psychologist had said, "We need to recognize that Peter Lawrence is right. The patient won't be healed until she can turn and face the truth—the pain. But," he continued, "the medical profession is dedicated to alleviating pain, not facing it. What we can offer is the use of drugs, such things as ECT, and supervision, but what we cannot do is to confront the pain."

Eventually my friend received a disability pension, and the medical staff told her she would not need to be reassessed. In other words, she was deemed incurable. So we sent her to some wonderful friends of ours at a place dedicated to Christian healing, and after a number of years of ministry in the power of the Holy Spirit, they asked the medical profession to examine her again. The medics could not believe what they were seeing. After more tests, they withdrew her disability pension and declared her fit for work. It is a wonderful story about the grace and healing of Jesus. She faced the pain in the power of the Spirit, assisted by the total commitment and expertise of those Christians.

Thomas

After the trauma of the Easter weekend, Jesus brought wholeness. He cared for His mother Mary (John 19:26–27). He "appeared to Simon" (Luke 24:34), Cleopas (Luke 24:18), and James (1 Cor. 15:7). Mary Magdalene had an emotional encounter with Him (John 20:17), holding onto Him and hugging Him. Jesus "stood among them and said, 'Peace be with you!'" (John 20:19). They were "overjoyed when they saw the Lord" (John 20:20). All were touched emotionally—but apparently not Thomas. He did not have a private meeting with Jesus; instead he struggled on alone. Thomas was not with the other ten disciples when Jesus ministered to them on Easter Sunday or when the others heard the words "receive the Holy Spirit" (John 20:22). He didn't get a personal visit.

Why was Thomas not there when Jesus appeared to the disciples? He may have just popped out to get some fish and chips for the group and simply missed the moment out of bad luck, but it doesn't read that way. More likely Thomas was not there because he chose not to be there. He wanted to be on his own to lick his wounds—to suffer alone. But Jesus did not restore Thomas privately.

When the others found Thomas, the good news that Jesus had been raised from the dead was not well received. Thomas did not believe or return to the fold immediately, and it looks as if it took a whole week for the doubting disciple to join the others (John 20:26). What a wonderful effort by the others to bring him back. Maybe in that week Jesus resisted the impulse to seek out Thomas on His own, knowing the emotional healing needed to happen in front of the others.

On the following Sunday, Thomas, encouraged by Jesus' presence, turned to face the pain—the key to emotional healing—with his friends. And what a healing! Jesus came through locked doors and stood among them, gave them His peace, showed them His hands and His side, and the doubter became a believer. And so it fell to Thomas to make the greatest declaration of belief in the New Testament: "My Lord and my God!" (John 20:28).

In the two upper room incidents after the resurrection, Jesus gives us a model, a virtual blueprint, for emotional healing. The suffering disciple turns to face the pain, confronts the trauma with Jesus, and in the presence of the body of Christ, declares Jesus as Lord, is filled with the Holy Spirit, and begins to walk out his healing by serving God.

What Was Happening When the Symptoms First Appeared?

On one occasion I went to minister to a middle-aged lady who had cancer and occasionally went to church. She'd had half her stomach removed, along with one or two other organs, and was not expected to live for more than about three or four weeks. I made an appointment to see her. The lady hadn't been out of bed for two or three months, but because I was coming, her caregivers prepared her and spent all morning getting her up and ready. She came down, dressed, into the lounge.

The question I asked was simple:

"What was happening in your life when the symptoms of the cancer first appeared?"

"I was promoted at work," she said immediately. "I did not want to be promoted but the supervisor left. I had been one of 'the girls' and people were very keen that I should have the job. They made me take it. So I took it but it didn't last very long. The cancer symptoms appeared within a few days, and eventually I left because I just couldn't cope with the pressure."

Noting that she lived in a very nice house and did not need the job, I asked another question: "Why did you go to work?"

"We didn't have any children, I had three miscarriages, we were told that we couldn't have children, neither of us wanted to adopt, so it was a question of needing something to do." She said she quite liked these people and enjoyed working for them.

First we asked the Holy Spirit to come to talk to her about the pressure of the job and the particular issue of being made to do something she did not want to do. I helped and encouraged her to repent of taking a job she never really wanted. Several times she said to me, "They made me take it." In this case she needed to repent of saying yes when she meant no and take the responsibility of her own actions in prayer.

Secondly, we addressed what seemed to me a very deep issue—not having any children, only miscarriages. So I asked, "How do you feel about the situation?" She said that they "did not have children" and that they "weren't parents." I said, "My understanding of the Christian faith is that once somebody has been created they have a spirit, and that spirit is made in the image of God. According to

Ecclesiastes, a spirit 'returns to God who gave it' when the person dies (Eccl. 12:7). Therefore you are parents, you do have children, they go to the presence of Jesus, and if we believe in the Lord Jesus, we shall see them one day."

This seemed to be something of a new idea to her, so I pushed it a bit further. I asked if they had named the children and given them to Jesus. "You could name them, admit you are parents, and say that you look forward to seeing them again."

Again this spoke to her, and I realized afterward this was a very significant spiritual moment—one of eternal importance. I was asking her to believe that these bits of matter that were flushed away were children, people who would live in eternity forever, and that she was their mother. She affirmed this truth gladly. For somebody who was not a great churchgoer, it was a momentous choice—a time to believe.

So we prayed. There were a lot of tears, we committed the children to Jesus, and for something like half an hour we asked the Spirit to come and do whatever He wanted to do. As she sat on the sofa, she wept and did serious business with God.

Eventually I said to her, "Having done some emotional healing, with the Lord, do you think you could now stand so that we can pray for physical healing as well?"

"Not on my own," she replied. So the two men on either side held her up and we asked the Holy Spirit to come and do physical healing.

He came very powerfully. She had never been to any of our meetings and was surprised to witness what now took place, as soon both her hands started shaking violently. This response embarrassed her.

"My hands can't stop shaking," she said.

"That's all right," I said. "That's the Holy Spirit. Just let Him come." So she just stood there as the Spirit came upon her in power. She shook for some time and eventually, when she opened her eyes again, sat down.

You could see the glow on her face, the presence of Jesus, the experience of power. I was hopeful. The whole thing was over in about an hour and then I left.

I think it was a Tuesday when we met with them and on Wednesday we had a meeting in church. She was there. She was there with her face shining. It was incredible. "Shall I pray for you again?" I asked.

"No," she replied, "I have come to pray for others." She did pray for others, she came to a few of our meetings, and during the next year she got to know Jesus very well. Her faith grew enormously and her new relationship with Jesus was there for all to see.

Sadly, after a year she died. I didn't pray with her again, and I am sorry I didn't, but I have been able to pass on to many other people what we learned together. Now we always ask people, "What was happening in your life when the symptoms first appeared?" It often leads to emotional healing that prepares people before we can then ask the Holy Spirit to heal them physically.

Simon Peter's Healing

The atmosphere in Mary's big house in Jerusalem was like a morgue. News had filtered through that Judas had hanged himself in the Valley of Hinnom, Jesus was dead and buried in a tomb near where they killed him, and no one was sleeping in the early hours of the morning. A piercing scream shattered the silence. "The body has gone!" screeched the woman's voice.

Peter and John ran to the tomb and found it was true, and later in the day Jesus appeared to Simon Peter alone.

"What was He like?" asked John.

"Different," replied his friend thoughtfully, "but the same." They chatted for a while without communicating very much until John asked a big question.

"Did He—you know—mention it?"

"No," said Peter, and then kept his thoughts to himself. Every time he saw Jesus after that, however, he was expecting it … in the upper room, a week later when Jesus confronted Thomas, when He taught them and ate with them, and even when He spoke to five hundred, but He never mentioned it once.

Eventually after five weeks John said, "I think you are okay now. I'm pretty sure He would have said something by now if He was going to."

Then one night, beside the shores of Galilee, seven of the disciples decided to go fishing. Thomas was now with them; they still had to eat and earn their keep, so they went out to catch what they could—and failed.

When they returned in the morning, Jesus stood on the beach and, as in several of His other appearances, they didn't recognize Him. "Caught any fish?" He asked, but the nets and baskets were all empty.

"Throw the nets on the other side of the boat," He said, and they obeyed. A big catch of fish provided enough for breakfast and alerted the disciples that it was the Lord.

The first time this miracle happened, Peter moved away from Jesus, but now he moved toward Him, now familiar with the presence of His holiness. After they had finished breakfast, Jesus asked Peter, "Do you love Me?"

"Of course," replied Peter.

"You are the shepherd," said the Lord. "Feed My lambs."

A second time He asked, "Do you love Me?"

"Of course," replied Peter.

"You are the shepherd," said the Lord. "Take care of My sheep."

A third time Jesus asked, "Do you love Me?" Peter finally understood, and it hurt.

Why did Jesus choose to hurt Peter? Because it was the only way he could heal from the trauma of the past, become free to serve Jesus in the future, and face the pain in the present—with Jesus. Peter denied Jesus three times and called down curses on his own head. It doesn't get much worse than that. When Jesus confronted him, all the ingredients needed for total healing, explicitly or implicitly, were present.

1. Peter declared his love for Jesus.
2. Jesus declared His love for Peter.
3. Jesus told Peter to be committed to the body of Christ.
4. Peter faced up to the pain of the past with Jesus.
5. Implicit in the whole action of restoration was forgiveness.
6. Jesus prepared Peter and informed him of things that must now happen.

"You are the shepherd," said Jesus for the third time. "Feed My sheep." Jesus helped Peter face the pain in front of some of the disciples and Himself, because He needed to restore Peter in view of those he would lead. Jesus healed him with the others, including Thomas, as witnesses.

Peter was now emotionally ready to take the gospel of Jesus into the world. It all came about because Jesus helped Peter to face the pain—leading him to get into touch with his feelings and to begin walking out his faith with Jesus in the power of the Holy Spirit. Simon Peter was now ready to take the gospel to the world, "ransomed, healed, restored, forgiven."[1]

A Word on a Train

One day I caught the train home from a ministry trip, and my eldest daughter Amanda was with me. When they were young, I enjoyed taking one of my daughters with me whenever I could, and our time together in the train playing board games and the like was very special. Then it happened.

"Peter, I want you to minister to that lady sitting over there." It was an unwelcome and intrusive thought. I couldn't see how it was possible. *Excuse me, madam, but I think the Lord is saying ...*

Others might be able to manage such intrusions into people's privacy on trains, but I certainly could not. Even so, I kept my eye on her during the rest of the journey.

Seated alone on the other side of the aisle, this rather overweight, middle-aged lady smoked continually and seemed to be registering some sort of distress on her face. Halfway to London she fell asleep. While she was sleeping, a man boarded the train, took his seat opposite her, and accidentally caught her foot with his. As he did so, she opened her eyes with a jump and looked "daggers-drawn" at him for a moment. After she closed her eyes again, I smiled at the man and we both shrugged our shoulders in recognition of one another's puzzlement at the incident.

If a word comes to me in a meeting, and it seems appropriate, I give it on the spot. I always introduce it with phrases such as—"Forgive me if I'm wrong but …" or "As we were worshipping, I wondered if the Lord might be saying …" It is then normally claimed or not and the whole incident has come and gone in five minutes. A possible word on a train is a different matter. As the wheels rattled over the lines and time passed by, the journey became more and more uncomfortable.

"Daddy, it's your turn again—you're not concentrating … don't you want to play Ludo with me?"

"Oh … er … yes … of course, dear. I still need a six, don't I?"

How could I minister to her? *Forgive my intrusion, madam, but would you mind standing up while I just lay my hands on you?*

Amanda's counters all arrived safely home while most of mine were still at base camp. I paused for a breather and realized we'd be there soon.

"Lord, just supposing this thought was from you," I prayed, "what should I do? It just doesn't seem possible."

"Trust Me," He said, and that was all.

Now if He had given me a message to pass on, or even a conversation-starter, I could maybe have had a go. *I saw you under a palm tree …* or *the man you're living with is not your husband …* or *been up any good sycamore trees lately?*

As we approached London, I instructed Amanda as clearly as possible about our connecting train, just in case we were accidentally parted. We had plenty of time.

The train came to a halt and I found myself standing next to the lady as we both sought to retrieve our baggage from the rack. "Are you all right?" I asked nonchalantly, and the lady obviously felt the need to explain the incident with the other passenger. She was suffering badly from a trapped nerve in her back. When the man caught her foot while sitting down, excruciating pain shot up the right-hand side of her body.

I commiserated, helped her off with her bags, and then turned my attention to Amanda and our suitcases. As we alighted from the train, the lady was struggling some distance ahead, obviously in pain, with no porters or trolleys to be seen.

Thoughts raced through my mind. A man cannot easily approach a woman he has never met before, on a busy London station, offering to pray for her. No, of course not, especially as I was not wearing my clerical collar. And yet there were extenuating circumstances. We had been in a train compartment together for over an hour, we had spoken, the platform was a public place, and I did have my daughter with me, which seemed to make a difference. She had seen me relating to my daughter for much of the journey, and I instinctively felt in this situation it would be possible. Somehow having Amanda with me made the whole idea of ministering much more within the bounds of social acceptability.

I asked the Lord what He thought and He had not changed His mind. I thought it might be appropriate, having already spoken to her, to say, "I'm a vicar, as you're in pain, would you like me to pray with you?" I could then hold my hands a few inches from the affected area and pray. There was still plenty of time before our next train was due to depart.

More thoughts jostled each other for prominence in my head as I suddenly realized I was well prepared for this moment. I am not often used for healing the sick, but I had previously prayed with three people in church with exactly the same condition as this lady; two had been instantly healed, and one had received much relief. The Lord did appear to have the right man on the spot! It didn't really matter if she was completely healed there and then as long as power came on her and she received some relief or positive experience in the name of Jesus. There were follow-up possibilities as well.

It so happened I had a few covers for a new book in my briefcase, having just had a meeting with my publisher. If I gave her one, this would tell her who I was, encourage her maybe to buy and read the Christian book, or perhaps write to me as my name and church were on the cover. I could then tell her all about Jesus and even suggest a nearby church. It was a situation with great potential. It is amazing how God can set up a divine appointment like this out of nothing.

About twenty yards in front of me the lady stopped, put her bags down, and held her pained back. I approached her gently, now knowing full well what God wanted me to do.

"Still having trouble?" I asked.

"Yes, I'm in agony," she said. "I don't know how I'm going to cope. I've still got to catch another train."

"Oh dear," I said. "I am sorry. Hope you manage," and went by on the other side.

"Thanks," she said.

Amanda and I walked on and left the lady behind with her bags and her pain.

In the next train I sat by the window. I looked into the glass and there, reflected before me with the clarity of a mountain stream in bright sunlight, was the mirror image of a discouraged failure who wanted to burst into tears, but didn't know how. Somebody else was there too.

"I'm still here, Peter," God appeared to say, "and I still love you." If anything this seemed to make it worse. I didn't want love. I didn't want forgiveness. I wanted to return to London and have another go.

"I can still heal her and bring her to Myself," I heard God say to the man in the window.

"I know, Lord," I eventually replied, "and I pray that You will. I'm just so sorry. How could I? After all I've preached and written, and desired for so long?"

God knew I didn't want an answer. I suppose that was it. Just another case of falling short. God's love came on me and I fell asleep. It seemed to be but a few moments before an excited voice startled me out of the security of my slumber.

"We're there!" exclaimed Amanda. Another time, another place, another chance to start again. The fount of Jesus' blood never runs dry. Carol's embrace and the hugs of my children felt very warm. Like Thomas and Peter, I needed to be healed emotionally by Jesus before I could give words from the Holy Spirit to change the world. Perhaps my failure, like those of Thomas and Peter, helped prepare me for what Jesus was about to do by His Spirit.

All I know is that if I am to share the gospel of Jesus, as the early disciples did, I regularly need Jesus to heal me emotionally, as He did with Mary, James, Cleopas, Mary Magdalene, Thomas, and Peter.

6

HEALING THE SICK

When I was in inner-city Birmingham, my life changed as the Holy Spirit worked through the American pastor John Wimber. When I arrived in rural Dorset, I found the churches in our area had been changed by the Holy Spirit working through another American pastor, Jean Darnell, and a number of other leaders. We have three churches in our parish, and three neighboring parishes are either "charismatic" or sympathetic to evangelical, charismatic teaching and practice. And that is just within the Church of England. (It's worth noting that, in Britain, many mainstream evangelical churches have embraced the charismatic movement to some degree.)

In our own three churches at Canford we still have people in our congregations who were saved, touched, and healed at Post Green, the home of Sir Tom and Lady Faith Lees, where Jean Darnell used to live and minister. In 1975 the baronet and his good lady allowed their home to become the center of a Christian community, but before then they had held meetings in the grounds of their estate with Jean as the speaker. For years people flocked from the Poole area of Dorset to this center of charismatic renewal, and in 2006, I was privileged to meet Sir Tom at a luncheon.

"We haven't met, Sir Tom," I began. "I'm the team rector at Canford Magna." He smiled knowingly and greeted me warmly. "Tell me about the Post Green Community," I ventured and then didn't have to speak for some time; he gave me the story enthusiastically. This is roughly what he said:

"Ken Prior (a local vicar) invited us to a meeting to hear an ordained lady minister from the Four Square Gospel Church who was an American called Jean Darnell. She was traipsing around Europe with her teenage daughter LaDonna in tow, while her husband, Elmer, was in Hong Kong, when she felt God had told her to do this. I felt sorry for them, as they had sold everything to come from America, so I invited them to come and stay at Post Green.

"Faith and I organized an evening meeting, did our best to get people there, and after we'd sung a hymn, Jean addressed the gathering.

"'Someone's being healed right now,' she said and then pointed to the side of the room by the fireplace. 'Over there. Whoever it is, stand up and receive your healing.'

"It was Dot Friend," explained Tom, knowing I knew her from one of Canford's three churches. "Dot had been suffering from severe bouts of hemorrhaging following the birth of her second child and this became much worse after the third was born. Dot was very weak because of it, couldn't climb the stairs, and hadn't been able to stand to sing the hymn that night. As Jean stood and spoke, Dot was completely healed. After that people flocked to our home."

Tom looked as though he had much more to say, paused, took a deep breath and then added, "I suppose we'd better go and have lunch now." So we did, but afterward I was inspired by our conversation to visit Dot. She filled in some details.

"Actually my healing began when I heard the Sisters of Mary from Darmstadt speaking at a conference a week before. The Spirit came powerfully upon me then and I found myself forgiving my brother for a wartime incident. This, I believe, opened me up to the possibility of Jesus healing me, but the meeting with Jean finished it all off and fully restored my energy.

"When we sang the words, 'Ponder anew what the Almighty can do,' I knew I was going to be healed. I couldn't stand like the others, but as Jean stood to speak, I felt this heat flooding through my body and I began to tingle all over. When Jean asked me to stand, I leapt out of the sofa. 'I'm not weak now,' I said. 'I'm healed!' And I danced about everywhere."

"Were others healed through Jean's ministry too?" I asked.

"Oh yes," she replied. "Mary was healed of a bad back at a later meeting."

So I checked that one out as well; I had just been on holiday with Mary and others from our church. Mary gave me the details.

"I was at this meeting in Post Green when Jean stood up to speak. 'The Lord is straightening out someone's tail bones,' she said. In my teens, during the War, I tripped and fell down some steps, injuring my spine, and over the years the resulting damage caused me increasing pain and difficulty. Dr. Morgan-Bill, my doctor and churchwarden at Canford, manipulated me, which eased it for a while, but by the time I was thirty, I couldn't sit down anywhere without being in pain. Apparently the tail bones were tucked right under."

Mary was advised to have an operation to remove the tailbones, but after Jean's word, she was found to be healed, surgery was no longer necessary, and forty years later she is still healed. Praise God.

A few years ago I bumped into Jean Darnell at a conference where we were both speaking.

"How are you, Jean?" I asked.

"Well. It's funny you should ask that, Peter," she replied. "I've just come out of hospital. I was booked in for a triple bypass operation on my heart when who do you think came to see me?"

"The Pope?" I suggested.

"Better than that," Jean answered with a smile. "Derek Prince. He'd heard I was ill and felt the Lord tell him to come and pray for me. He was returning to America from Spain and broke his journey at Heathrow."

"And?" I asked with a smile of my own, afraid I might not get the rest of the details.

"He laid hands on me, of course, and I was discharged the next day without an operation. Here I am."

It isn't necessary to have a special word from God before He can heal us, but it often helps. Over the years we have found a word from the Spirit of God to be of enormous value for encouraging, receiving, and keeping Jesus' healing, in many different ways. It has helped us to follow the biblical pattern we see in operation as Jesus healed the sick in the Gospels, guided and empowered by the Holy Spirit.

Most of the different ways the Spirit helps us can be found in Luke 5:17–26, in which Jesus heals a paralyzed man, and I have found these five principles to be of great value: love, authority, power, discernment, and faith.

Love

Mark begins his version of this story by saying: "A few days later, when Jesus again entered Capernaum, the people heard that he had come home" (Mark 2:1). It looks as though this was Jesus' home. Matthew 4:13 says, "Leaving Nazareth, [Jesus] went and lived in Capernaum" (cf. Matt. 9:1). It seems as if the house that was crowded out with teachers of the law and Pharisees was Jesus' cottage by the sea, where His mother and brothers used to come and stay, and the roof that the four men smashed up was His own (John 2:12). He'd probably built it Himself, being practical and good at carpentry.

After a busy time Jesus came home for a rest, only to be interrupted by important people who'd come all the way from Jerusalem to argue with Him. He was in the middle of a tense time that required His full concentration when, suddenly, vandals broke into His home. My reaction in such circumstances would probably have been unprintable—Jesus' reaction was one of love. If anyone had felt before this incident that they couldn't disturb Jesus with their problems because He was too well known, too tired, or too busy, they would have had to think again. When the poor and the needy turned to Jesus for help, He always met them with love.

Love is a natural healer. If a child cries out with a toothache in the night, a loving touch from Mom or Dad will often alleviate the pain. In *The Go-Between God,* Bishop John V. Taylor wrote: "More and more practitioners are coming to recognize that the little-known dynamics of our interpersonal relations are the clue to a great deal of healing. We are rediscovering the therapy of touch, which is a sacrament of acceptance and love."[1]

When Christians listen to sick people, spend time with them, pray with them, and lay hands lovingly on them—whatever else happens—they should always feel loved. Sometimes, however, a word from the Spirit can help the sick person feel especially loved by God.

One Friday at lunchtime I entered the kitchen joyously with a newly written sermon, hoping to receive spiritual encouragement and physical sustenance. Unfortunately my wife, Carol, was absent, putting our youngest to bed, and I was left alone with my needs. I put a record of Stainer's *Crucifixion* on the turntable, reclined in an easy chair with my eyes closed, and at once a wave of warmth came over me. A tear slid down my cheek, and I sensed the presence of God with me by His Spirit in a special way.

In my mind I saw Jesus in a children's book picture of the garden of Eden, but there was no serpent present. "This is My world," Jesus said lovingly. "Do not be afraid." For some time almost every moment of every day had been taken up ministering to demonized people and it seemed good to spend time apart with Jesus and rest for a while, in a beautiful garden without snakes. I was due to travel that afternoon to Cheltenham to take some seminars on healing in another church.

"When you go to Cheltenham this weekend," Jesus said, "I want you to know everything you receive in your mind will be of Me, and I will bless all who come. There will be thirty there, and here are some words to help you." On the newspaper lying on the floor, I jotted down these words:

Bone displacement—hip.
Lady with blurred vision in left eye.

Bladder complaint.

Epilepsy.

Each of the meetings had a different number in attendance, ranging from twenty-four to thirty-three, but on the afternoon when I felt it right to give the four words, thirty people were present, and all the words were claimed. A lady was suffering from pain in the hip due to the bone continually slipping out of place, and as people laid hands on her, the pain left. Another lady began to see more clearly in the left eye as friends in Christ prayed over her, and yet another lady with a minor bladder complaint was grateful for prayer that eventually concentrated on her more serious emotional problems.

Rob had epilepsy. Thirty years before, he had been preparing to enter the ordained ministry when he had an accident and fell twenty feet onto his head. His wife was told he would not live more than a couple of hours, but as she drove to the hospital, she sensed the Spirit saying he would survive, and he did. Unfortunately the operation on his brain left him with epilepsy, causing him to abandon plans for the ordained ministry and remain unemployed for the rest of his working years. In all that time he and his wife kept their faith in God, but not once at any of the meetings they attended was he ever called out to the front by a special word for prayer. The word "epilepsy" had never featured at healing meetings Rob attended, until our Cheltenham weekend.

As we prayed for him, he was overcome with God's love. It seemed almost too much for Rob that the Holy Spirit had given a special word just for him. Heat came upon his head, and it fell backward under the Spirit's power as a tear or two trickled down his face, just as they had on mine the previous day. Rob had no more fits for some time, but maybe the most important thing after so many years was the special love I know he felt from God. A special word from the Holy Spirit often helps the sick and needy to feel His great love for them.

Authority

Having suffered a hole in his roof, Jesus then faces an atmosphere of skepticism and antagonism from those who challenge His authority. Before He heals the paralytic, Jesus says, "But that you may know that the Son of Man has authority …" (Luke 5:24).

Jesus demonstrates His authority to forgive sins by healing the crippled man, simultaneously proving His authority to heal the sick. We need to be sure we have the authority of God to heal the sick. I have found that, in addition to the general authority that can be seen in Scripture, there is also particular authority that can come with a word from God.

Margery, from Wimborne in Dorset, suffered very badly from multiple sclerosis. It crept up on her from the early age of eighteen until, several years later, she became paralyzed. Her legs were useless, and she had to be lifted from bed to a wheelchair and strapped round with belts to keep her from falling forward. Her parents needed to feed her, as she had no control over the spoon. Since she had no power in her left arm, her mother also needed to cut up her daughter's food into small pieces. Margery's left eye was completely closed, and the right eye often had treble vision, so she wore dark glasses to try to help the sight of the one eye. From time to time she suffered from blackouts and would lose consciousness for hours. Despite all of this, Margery loved the Lord Jesus and never lost faith in Him or His Word.

One February night Margery had a dream of herself sitting in her chair beside the bed, putting out her left leg. As she awoke to discover it was only a dream, she heard a voice saying, "Tarry a little longer." Bravely Margery told several of her praying friends about it and, though her condition worsened, her faith that Jesus was going to heal her strengthened. Her speech, however, continued to deteriorate until she could no longer make herself understood.

Five months after the dream, when she was now totally helpless in every way, her husband said good-bye to her at five to six in the morning. At six fifteen her mother brought her a cup of tea. At six twenty Margery's father and mother lifted her from the bed, strapped her in the chair beside the bed, put a bell in her good hand, and left her alone.

While her father went upstairs to find a towel and her mother went to get her washing water, Margery felt a warm glow come all over her body. Her left foot, which was doubled up, straightened out—just as in the dream—and the toes of the right foot, which were pointed toward the heel, came back into position.

Margery grasped the handle of her bedroom door, which was beside her, undid the straps that were about her body, and said, "By faith in Jesus I will stand." Having stood for a while, to make sure she could, the former paralytic sat down, rang the bell, and called out with clear articulation for her parents. They came running, fearing the worst.

"Take my hands, Mum," she said. "Don't be afraid. Something wonderful has happened." She put out her right arm, and as she did

so, her left arm came out from behind her and joined the other one. A
few minutes later she tried on her wedding ring and found it fit for the
first time in years as her thin fingers had now increased to normal size.
Her mother said, "How wonderful. Your hand is warm and well again."
Margery replied, "It's more wonderful than that, Mum. I can stand."

Holding her mother's hands, she stood and declared, "I'm walking with God." Unaided, Margery then walked from her bedroom,
through the small dining room to the kitchen, while her parents
trailed mutely behind.

When Margery returned to the dining room, she took off her
glasses and said, "If I can trust God for my hands and feet, I can
trust Him for my sight." In a moment, in the twinkling of an eye, the
left one opened, and her sight was fully restored. Afterward Margery
wrote, "Jesus made such a perfect job that I do not now need the
glasses I had before I was ill, and I am able to write dozens of letters
a day. To him be all the glory!"

Later, Dr. Hugh Morgan-Williams, "Morgan-Bill," the churchwarden of Canford Magna, examined Margery. He confirmed the
miracle, as did many other nurses and doctors who saw her. After
this, for many years Margery Stevens spoke in churches and fellowship meetings giving her testimony, and always gave all the glory to
Jesus. Sometimes a word from the Spirit of God can increase our
faith to receive and claim the authority He gives us for healing at a
particular time in a particular place.

Power

Luke records that on the occasion when the four men lowered their
paralyzed friend through the roof, Jesus not only had God's authority

but also His power to heal the man: "And the power of the Lord was present for [Jesus] to heal the sick" (Luke 5:17).

At healing meetings, services, and conferences, there are times when God's healing power is manifested for all to see; they are very precious moments indeed and need to be treasured.

For two years Sharon suffered badly from postviral chronic fatigue syndrome, fibromyalgia, and irritable bowel syndrome, spending a lot of time at home unable to do anything. She used a wheelchair due to extreme pain and fatigue.

In May 2007, Sharon went away with our St. Barnabas church for a weekend at the Sidholme conference center in Devon with her husband, Mike (our church treasurer), and son Philip. On Friday evening, the pain in her hands had been extremely bad, which was upsetting because Sharon likes to draw but couldn't hold a pen without excruciating pain.

At the end of the meeting on Friday night, people were invited to come to the front for prayer, and Sharon wheeled forward with others. Geoff, the team vicar of St. Barnabas, and his wife, Teresa, prayed for her, and without knowing the latest situation, Geoff asked if he could hold her wrists. This was what he felt the Lord wanted him to do.

When anyone suffers from a chronic illness, they often receive a lot of prayer from their church, and after a while it is easy to lose heart. What they need in a situation like this is a little sign from God that He knows, understands, and is on their case. Geoff's leading from the Lord to take hold of Sharon's wrists was just such a sign to her at a time when the pain in her hands and wrists was her biggest problem and greatest fear. Not being able to draw would have felt like the end for Sharon, who is a talented artist.

A second sign came as Geoff and Teresa prayed. Power came on Sharon's hands and wrists in the form of pins and needles. The Spirit of God was doing something; Sharon shared this with Geoff and Teresa, who then offered prayers for her with expectancy and faith.

A third sign happened the following day. Sharon wrote this to me:

> On Saturday during the session the Lord gave me
> several pictures and I drew them without any pain.
> It was wonderful.

The evening, however, was not so wonderful. The St. Barnabas fellowship decided to have a ceilidh, which is the sort of thing they do—they are a fun group with a Lancashire leader. A ceilidh is an informal evening of song, story, and dancing, particularly popular in Scotland and Ireland. Sharon hated not being able to join in and became extremely depressed and frustrated. She asked Michael to take her back to their room.

Mike returned to the party. Alone with God, Sharon told Him a thing or two that she felt He needed to hear. He already knew, but it probably did her good to express it. Everything seemed so unfair.

That night Sharon had a strange dream. She was very busy preparing for the coming of Jesus, knowing she had to get ready, but she was so busy that Jesus came and went and Sharon missed Him. In the dream she was devastated; when she awoke she didn't understand the meaning of it, and wondered what God was doing or saying, if anything.

At the final session of the weekend away, on Sunday morning, Sharon sensed the Spirit tell her to get out of the chair, so she did, and stood up. Hilary came to her and started to pray for her, as did Dot, of Post Green fame, who was standing behind her. Hilary then stopped and asked Sharon what she was afraid of.

"Being made well," she whispered, "and the consequences. Going back to everything. Working, looking after the family, losing the benefits, coping with people's reaction. Will they say I am a fraud and it's all been just an act?"

They prayed again, gave it all over to God, and the pain left. Sharon went to the front with one of her pictures and said to Teresa, "Jesus has healed me. I'm healed." This was followed by as much whooping, hollering, hugging, and praising God as South Coast Anglicans could manage, and everyone joined in except Sharon's husband, Mike. He was out in the Spirit at the time, lying on the floor, and he missed it all. But everyone else witnessed Sharon walking around and blessing the entire gathering.

Sharon Raymond went to Sidholme in a wheelchair and came home walking. When she saw the doctor and told him Jesus had healed the fibromyalgia, he didn't believe her. Doctors can be like that. He had her do some exercises and movements she hadn't been able to do before and checked over the joint swellings that had now disappeared. "How do I write up your notes scientifically?" he asked. "Just put that Jesus healed me," she said. The next time she went to see him, the doctor sang "Hallelujah!" (the George Frideric Handel version) as she walked through the door.

And the dream? Several months later Sharon was trying to go back to her old ways. Stressing over finances, fussing about the house, being too busy, and tiring herself out, but whenever she sat down exhausted, the Spirit always said the same thing to her: "Remember the dream." From time to time the Holy Spirit speaks to help us keep our healing, as well as to be healed.

In May 2007 the power of the Lord was present in Sidholme for Jesus to heal Sharon from the chronic fatigue and fibromyalgia. In September He healed her irritable bowel problem when Laurie, from one of our neighboring churches, visited St. Barnabas and prayed with Sharon. The following day when Sharon prayed and asked the Lord why the healing had not been completed in Sidholme, He reminded her of His word to give up her job, which she hadn't done. Immediately Sharon handed in her notice, and now she works for me as my assistant, which is, of course, a thrill and a joy that involves no stress at all. To God be all the glory!

Discernment

When the four friends lowered the paralyzed man through the roof, Jesus spoke to him. Luke records it like this: "When Jesus saw their faith, he said, 'Friend, your sins are forgiven'" (Luke 5:20). This is an amazing statement. A more logical account would have read, "When Jesus saw their faith, He said, 'Get up, take your mat, and go home.'"

Presumably Jesus discerned that the man needed to have his sins forgiven before being healed. Maybe he was a bad sinner; maybe people had accused him of being a bad sinner because he was crippled; maybe he had a low self-image and thought he was a bad sinner; maybe Jesus needed to forgive him in order to heal him; maybe Jesus needed to forgive him so that he might know how to keep his healing afterward. Whatever the reason, Jesus discerned the need for forgiveness before He healed him. I suspect this was revealed to Him supernaturally, for they were the first words in the conversation.

I can find no other instance in the Gospels where Jesus forgave someone's sins before healing the sickness, which suggests the presence of a spiritual problem. Once we have welcomed a sick person with love, received authority to pray, and sensed the anointing of the Lord's presence to heal the sick, we too may need spiritual discernment as to how to minister.

It was hot in the warehouse. Very hot. The young man was packing copies of my first book, *The Hot Line,* for distribution to the bookshops. As the day wore on, a bad headache developed that caused him to stop and sit down.

"Help, Lord!" he prayed. "I'm trying to do Your work but I don't think I can carry on with this headache."

"Open one of the books you are packing," said the Holy Spirit into his mind, with an inner conviction in his spirit, "and see what it says."

So, completely at random, he took a copy of *The Hot Line*, opened it, put his finger in it, and read: "It's only a demon."

"Thank you, Lord," he said as he shut the book and put it back.

"Demon of Satan," he commanded, "in the name of Jesus, come out!"

Tension rose up inside him, he coughed a bit, then yawned, and as peace settled all over him, he realized the headache had gone. He returned at once to his packing and very kindly sent me this account. Sometimes the Holy Spirit gives us the spiritual discernment we need before we can be healed.

Faith

Jesus began His ministry to the sick man "when [He] saw their faith" (Luke 5:20). Faith can be present in the person ministering

(Luke 7:11–17; 22:50–51), in the sick person (Mark 5:25–34; Acts 14:8–10), or in some other person or friends (Matt. 8:5–13), but faith in God and His power and willingness to heal through Jesus by His Spirit normally needs to be present for God to supernaturally heal someone.

Receiving the Gift of Faith

How do we come by faith? How did the four friends who lowered the paralytic through the roof receive their faith? The implication in Mark's gospel is that a crowd gathered because of what had happened in Capernaum a few days earlier: "That evening after sunset the people brought to Jesus all the sick and demon-possessed. The whole town gathered at the door, and Jesus healed many who had various diseases" (Mark 1:32–34). So the whole town had already seen Jesus heal the sick. At the very least I suspect these four friends had seen Jesus healing people, but sick people did not normally have many able-bodied friends. One wonders if the four had themselves been among the sick whom Jesus healed a few days before and had now decided to bring their friend to Jesus.

The Faith of Friends

In recent years we have held special meetings in Canford Magna Parish Church on Sunday evenings in August. These meetings have been packed. In 2006, ninety-four-year-old Amelia, whom I know well and who lives nearby, shared with us how the Holy Spirit had healed her on three separate occasions.

At the age of five Amelia was rushed to the hospital suffering from meningitis and pneumonia. The surgeons performed a rib resection to release the pus from the lung, but later sent for her parents to say she was dying, and they could do no more. In those days there weren't any antibiotics.

Amelia's grandfather was preaching in Switzerland at the time, so her parents sent him a cable asking for prayer. Having listened first to the Holy Spirit, as he always did, Grandpa got the two thousand people in the congregation to hold hands and make a prayer chain, right around the church, up the stairs, and into the gallery while he prayed over a handkerchief (Acts 19:12). He sent it back to England, and as soon as the handkerchief touched the little girl's pillow, she began to recover and within a very short time was completely healed. From then on whenever her doctor saw her playing in the street, he called her "the miracle child."

Like Jesus, Amelia's grandfather only did what he saw the Father doing, and the handkerchief he felt led to use became a focal point for his friends' faith in Jesus.

Faith in Those Ministering

Faith can also be aroused in the person ministering by a word from God. Ananias heard the Lord speaking in a vision, telling him to go and lay hands on Saul, who was blind (Acts 9:1–19). He knew about Saul and argued, but the Lord said "Go!" so he went (v. 15). As Ananias laid hands on his head, "immediately, something like scales fell from Saul's eyes, and he could see again" (v. 18). Hearing God speak like this can be a tremendous faith-builder.

Complete deafness struck Amelia at the age of eleven. It lasted for two years, during which time prayers for her condition did not bring any healing. The family went on holiday to London and stayed at a hotel in Sussex Square. One morning after breakfast, Grandpa read out loud in the lounge from his Bible. Everyone there at the time heard every word, whether they wanted to or not, except Amelia.

After the Bible reading, her grandfather sensed the Spirit speaking to him, walked into the foyer, told everyone to stop talking, and promptly pulled Amelia into the center of a group of unknown visitors. In front of them all he placed his hands on her ears and prayed for healing, but his granddaughter still did not hear or feel a thing.

In the afternoon Amelia went along with the family to hear Grandpa preaching in Kingsway Hall, despite her continued deafness. It was what they did when on holiday. As he opened his Bible, and everyone present opened theirs, the eleven-year-old heard such a rustle of pages from all around the hall that she said out loud, "I can hear." Amelia still loves the rustle of the Bible's pages in meetings today, people opening God's Word, and can still hear clearly without a hearing aid.

Grandpa's name was Smith Wigglesworth. He sensed this was the moment the Holy Spirit was choosing to heal his granddaughter, and she was healed. His faith for healing in Jesus' name always stemmed from reading the Bible and listening to the Father in the power of the Holy Spirit.

The Sick Person's Faith

> In Lystra there sat a man crippled in his feet, who was lame from birth and had never walked. He listened to Paul as he was speaking. Paul looked directly at him, saw that he had faith to be healed

and called out, "Stand up on your feet!" At that, the
man jumped up and began to walk. (Acts 14:8–10)

Faith seemed to come to this man as he heard the word of God
being preached, and he believed. It is never easy for a sick person to
have faith for healing, which is why a word from God can be so helpful.

Not surprisingly, as Amelia grew up, her faith in Jesus stayed
with her. In 1931, when she was a junior nurse in Leeds, an accident
caused a scalpel to slip into her right thumb. The sister was very cross
and said, "We'll put a dressing on it, you can find some clean gloves,
and then get on with your work—we don't think about ourselves in
hospital." The next day the thumb was swollen so Amelia reported
off sick—for eleven months.

During this time she had seven operations, and the last one was
performed by one of the King's own surgeons from London. Before
he did so, however, he took hold of her hand and said, "Lassie, I will
do my best but I may have to amputate your hand."

Amelia kept her hand, but the wound would not heal and went
on discharging pus. That was when she remembered her grandfather was coming to the Preston Convention at Easter. She asked the
medical superintendent if she could go but was refused permission
to leave the hospital, even though she had not been able to work as a
nurse for eleven months.

This was a big test of faith. Amelia sensed that if she went, the
Holy Spirit would heal her; but if He didn't heal her, there would
be big trouble following her disobedience. In the end it felt like a
choice between human authority and God's authority, so Amelia
chose God and went to the convention on Good Friday, without her

grandfather knowing she was there. On this occasion it would be *her* faith in Jesus, rather than his, that would lead to healing.

Smith asked all who wanted to be healed to stand and Amelia stood with five hundred others. "If you believe God can do it," he said, "put one hand up," and his granddaughter's hand went up. He then prayed for wholesale healing. "If you believe God has healed you," Smith went on, "put the other hand up," and Amelia's second hand was one of many that went up.

Afterward, when the dressing was taken off, she said, "Look, I'm healed." The thumb was closed and healed and a piece of dead bone that had caused the trouble was lying in the gauze.

The medical superintendent was very annoyed until he saw the evidence of her healing. After that, whenever he saw Amelia, often at a distance, he held up his thumb in her direction, with a smile on his face. This story shows that God sometimes arouses faith for healing in the sick person.

When the paralytic's friends brought him to Jesus, He received them with love; Jesus knew in His spirit He had the authority to heal the man; He sensed the power of the Holy Spirit was present for Him to heal the sick; He discerned in the Spirit that He needed to offer the sick man the forgiveness of sins; He recognized the faith of those who had come to Him, and told the man to get up and walk. The man obeyed and was healed. I believe that hearing the Spirit speak to us today can help us do what Jesus did. There were opposing forces in Jesus' case, and in Amelia's, too, but if we hold our nerve and obey the Spirit's prompting, we can see the love of God break powerfully into people's lives.

7

SETTING THE CAPTIVES FREE

I was sitting in my study trying to think of things not to do when I noticed a police lady in our garden. She'd come in by the side gate behind the garage where no one could see her and was surreptitiously knocking on a door that hadn't been used for years. With great difficulty I found the key for the door and a can of oil, and let her in.

"Strictly off the record, vicar," she began, "please don't tell anyone at the station, but I wondered if you could help us?" Of course—anything I could do—I was just so relieved to discover it wasn't my vehicle tax or the state of my tires that had brought on the visit. And then this strange tale unfolded.

At a house in our parish lived a married couple with two children. He was a big, tough, man's man type of bloke who went to the pub every night with his mates while his wife stayed at home to look after the kids.

One night, while he was out, a bit of a brick came through the back window, followed by another, and another, smashing several panes of glass. The police came, found nothing, and went away again. The couple repaired the window, but the same incident happened again and again. The man stopped going to the pub, but the stones and broken bricks kept coming, as did the police, and their visits seemed to stir the missiles into greater activity.

While several constables stood in the back garden, debris made up mainly of stones and bricks flew at lightning speed over their heads, smacked into the windows behind them, and destroyed whatever bits of glass were still left. Soon all the downstairs windows facing the garden were boarded up.

"This has been going on now for several weeks," said our lady beat bobby. "We never see anything, our infrared cameras never reveal anything, the people in the house are scared stiff, and it's costing us thousands of pounds in surveillance. Do you think you might be able to help?"

Clearly the police lady came to visit me because she wondered if it was a spiritual problem rather than a physical one. At this time in my life I knew virtually nothing about the demonic, but if we were in the realm of supernatural activity, I did know Jesus was the answer. I knew I would need a word or two from the Holy Spirit in order to take this opportunity now presented to me. I asked a few trusted church members to pray, asked the Holy Spirit to show me what to do, and made the decision to do whatever He said. I felt His instructions were clear.

1. Get Spirit-filled friends to cover my visit to the family with prayer.
2. Be guided in the situation as to whether the family members were the source of this activity or its victims.

3. If I discerned that the problem rested with the family, I would need to help them to turn to Jesus.
4. If they were the victims, I still believed God wanted me to offer Jesus as the answer.
5. In short, the Lord said, "It is a spiritual problem and Jesus is the solution."

The victims' home was an ordinary terrace house occupied by an ordinary Birmingham couple. I looked carefully around the lounge for anything dodgy—occult magazines, weird pictures, pornographic or violent videos, upside-down crosses, etc.—but spotted nothing.

They repeated the story and showed me the boarded-up windows that once had panes of glass in them. Yes, it was still going on, so I asked a lot of Sherlock Holmes–type questions until finally the Spirit highlighted a possible source of the trouble. It all started when the old man next door had died, and he was a bit strange. What could I offer? Well ... Jesus actually ... that's what vicars are about.

I decided to tell them about Jesus and His offer to be with us today by His Holy Spirit, and I think at that stage, they'd have tried anything and anyone.

"You have authority over your own home, garden, and bodies," I said. "If you are willing to invite Jesus into your home, your garden, and yourselves, then I am prepared to ask Him to come."

They were willing, and that is what I did. I went with them into every room in the house. In the name of Jesus I commanded anything evil to leave and invited the Holy Spirit to come and dwell there. I did the same in the garden and then one by one I laid hands on mum, dad, and the two children, and asked Him to come to them with His peace.

During the whole visit I saw nothing, heard nothing, smelled nothing, and experienced nothing. I believed the police lady's story and the couple's confirmation of it, and I believed in the power of Jesus Christ over all evil. After I prayed, I told them it might get worse or it might get better, but to feel free to call me again if they needed me. They never did.

A couple of months later I bumped into them in the street, and we stopped to chat. No, there had not been one single stone or brick since my visit, and there was no more fear in the house or any of the occupants. They had not been to church once since then to thank Jesus, or me, but the power of Jesus was fully demonstrated in that dad was now back at the pub every night with his mates.

This couple never did come to church, write, or ring me. I was like the gasman or the television repairman. If bricks and stones smash all your windows, and the police can't fix it, call the vicar. Unlike the gas and television men though, the vicar comes free.

Finding Demons

In the heart of the Old Testament we read that Job "was blameless and upright; he feared God and shunned evil" (Job 1:1). Satan destroyed his sons and daughters and possessions and "afflicted Job with painful sores from the soles of his feet to the top of his head" (Job 2:7). Job's comforters did not recognize the work of Satan and, although Job protested his innocence, they added to his suffering with their false accusations.

Just as Job faced attacks from Satan, the Bible and experience suggest that Christians and non-Christians can undergo demonic affliction today. Failing to discover demons, to discern their activity, and deal with them, can leave people suffering as Job suffered. Job's comforters did their best with the revelation God had given them, but we who live on the other side of the cross have access to the power of the Spirit and the mind of Christ (1 Cor. 2:10–16). I believe that hearing the Spirit speak can help us to find demons and deal with them much more easily than was possible in Old Testament days.

The Gerasene demoniac did not go looking for Jesus; the Good Shepherd came and found him (Luke 8:26–39). Jesus crossed a stormy sea to find him and set him free. I suspect Jesus was doing what the Father was doing. As Jesus sailed toward the demon-possessed man, a mighty wind came on the sea, like the mighty wind that killed Job's family, and Jesus rebuked it in much the same way that He often rebuked demons. (The same Greek word is used.) Sometimes when we are on the way to do deliverance or to find demons, the enemy has a go at us and we need to be ready. But doing what the Father is doing is always our greatest protection and greatest joy.

One Sunday afternoon I was preparing and praying prior to speaking at a healing service that evening. "Tonight," God seemed to say, "I want you to look for a demon and cast it out." This was very strange, as I generally teach people to do deliverance midweek, unless there are exceptional reasons, not at meetings, but I noted it. *How do you find a demon anyway?* I wondered.

People from our church were coming with me, but as they had not yet arrived, I took a walk around the outside of our church. We'd been suffering from vandalism in the garden of remembrance, so I went around the back of the church on my own to check out the area. There was nobody there and no signs of trouble, but on the grass was a brand-new "girlie magazine." I picked it up, as I obviously didn't want it to stay there, but found myself flicking through a couple of pages. They didn't have things like that when I was a teenager, and I was curious, but as soon as I glimpsed what was in there, I sensed what was happening, put the magazine in my pocket, took it to Carol, and asked her to destroy it. Then I pondered over the incident.

Coincidence? On my way to a healing meeting? Been told to look for a demon. Could it be that what was obviously a temptation could also be a clue? I noted it.

When I arrived at the church, I made sure there was a room available for private ministry, just in case I had heard the Spirit of God correctly, and the service then proceeded as planned. When the ministry time drew to a close, I wondered how I was expected to find a demon. Maybe I would see the word *demon* written on someone's forehead? I searched in vain and was about to avail myself of a cup of tea when one of our team asked me to assist in ministering to a lady with a pain in the head. This pain had arrived only after we had welcomed the Holy Spirit and intensified when people sought to minister to her in the name of Jesus. *Ah,* I thought. *People don't normally get headaches when we ask the Holy Spirit to come. It normally works the other way round.*

When I saw the lady in question, all kinds of other alarm bells went off in me. She was dressed completely in black, in a short miniskirt, fishnet tights, and a completely see-through blouse and was sitting in the front row. *Not quite the dress I would expect at a*

Sunday-night healing service in an Anglican church, I thought. *And to sit in the front row? Nobody sits in the front row in the Church of England.*

This is the stage in helping people, especially those who may be demonized, that always requires sensitivity and love. I followed my Spirit-filled intuition, as it had been a powerful meeting, and backed the word that had come to me earlier. Consequently I invited her to come to the private room with me, together with a woman from our ministry team. I would not normally take someone out of a meeting where a lot of other ministry is taking place just for a physical condition, but this seemed the safest thing to do in case this was the lady the Spirit had spoken to me about. She was pleased to come.

There was no need at this point to declare what I thought the Spirit had said to me. We were still trying to deal with a headache, and so naturally I discussed the possible causes of the physical pain. As she suggested a particular reason for her problem, the thought formed in my mind, "She's not telling you the whole truth; she needs to repent." As it transpired, this was a word from the Holy Spirit to me about the situation, but it was not easy at that stage to know how to use such information while ministering. I waited prayerfully after she had finished speaking, and the Spirit convicted her in the silence. I hardly needed to say, "Are you sure that is all?" for immediately after I finished she poured the truth out to us and repented of her sins.

It turned out that she had received some similar ministry for the same problem before, and she was able to tell us that the name of the demon was "Lust." I think I might have guessed that one. I asked God to send His Holy Spirit in power on the headache, and as I did so, the pain intensified. I looked into her eyes and commanded the demon of lust to go in Jesus' name. There was a mild belch, and the headache went. We continued ministering for a while in prayer as God's peace and blessing came powerfully upon her.

Hearing the Spirit speak can sometimes help us to discern the presence of demons.

Finding the Entry Point

It seems to me that people cannot catch demons like measles. Demons can afflict and damage us as Satan harmed Job, but I don't think they can enter and reside in people unless some door has been opened through sin. It may be the person's own sin (Rev. 9:20) or sin done to them by someone else (Ps. 106:37) or their ancestors' sin (Ex. 34:7; Deut. 23:3–4), but just as the Holy Spirit moves most freely in righteousness, so demons appear to thrive on sin.

In 1 Samuel 15, King Saul disobeys God by not killing enough sheep, and Samuel says to him, "Rebellion is as the sin of witchcraft" (1 Sam. 15:23 NKJV). After this, God withdraws His blessing from Saul, and an evil spirit continues to trouble him.

Often it is as though demons leave by the same door through which they entered. Discovering the entry point and dealing with it through repentance and forgiveness help us open the door and remove demons more easily.

We had trouble ministering to a lady who experienced extreme physical pain and discomfort whenever we asked God to send His Spirit upon her. There were circulation and breathing problems and severe pain in various parts of the body, especially the heart and brain. We ministered three times when this happened, and at the end of each session a demon appeared to leave, but we could not continue in this way because of the physical distress.

Graham, the vicar from my next-door parish, was sharing this ministry with me, and on the third occasion he received a picture from the Spirit of some pigs in a pen behind a gate that was firmly shut. It seemed to him we were simply dragging the occasional pig out through the railings of the fence, when we really needed to find out how to open the gate to release them all. Recognizing the pigs to be the demons, Graham advised the lady to pray on her own to see if the Spirit of God would reveal the gate to her. This was a picture given by God for a particular situation, but I have also found it a helpful truth that applies to many situations. It is not easy getting pigs out through railings, and if a person exhibits excessive distress and pain when demons leave, it is often worth stopping and looking prayerfully for the gate.

The next day, when alone, the lady asked the Holy Spirit to come and spent the whole day weeping for the death of her grandfather, who had died when she was four years old. This was unexpected because she imagined she had something much more traumatic to be grieving over. From the age of seven she'd been a victim of abuse almost until she was married, and other horrific things had happened to her as a teenager—it therefore seemed surprising that an ordinary bereavement could cause such a problem. But her grandfather was the only one she felt had ever really loved her, and he had brought her up for the first four years of her life. No one ever told her properly about his death, and from then on she lived in a world of her own, talking to an imaginary person at the bottom of the garden to compensate for the awful feelings of loss and rejection. The imaginary person was not holy, and turning to an unclean spirit for comfort had opened the door to troublesome demons.

Two days later we had a Christian nurse who helped us, leading her through a time of saying good-bye to Granddad. Again there was quite an emotional response, and after this the lady was ready to repent of turning to demons for help rather than Jesus. Once she repented, and turned to Jesus alone for help and comfort, the demons almost fell over each other to come out. Many appeared to leave that day without causing anything like the anguish of a few days before.

A direct word from the Spirit may reveal the entry point through which demons enter, enabling us to reopen the gate and drive them out. Finding such a gate often makes casting out demons a much easier and less painful process.

Finding the Identity

Jesus appears to have known the identity of most of His spiritual enemies. In the wilderness He commanded Satan to go by name, and he left (Matt. 4:10–11); He asked Legion his name (Mark 5:9; Luke 8:30); He cast out a "deaf and mute spirit" (Mark 9:25); and a demon that was mute (Luke 11:14); He dealt with a demon that caused a man to be blind and dumb (Matt. 12:22); and He recognized that "a daughter of Abraham" whom He healed had been crippled by a spirit for eighteen years (Luke 13:11, 16).

Although Jesus was in His very nature fully God and fully man, the Gospels present Him as a man filled with the Spirit, anointed for ministry, meaning we can do even "greater things" (John 14:12) as we continue that ministry. It may have been a gift of discernment that enabled Jesus to recognize a demon or its manifestations in the person, or it may have been a direct word from God in His spirit, but Jesus did seem to know the identity of demons on a number of occasions, and not all were immediately obvious. He certainly knew what they did and how to get rid of them.

In the story recorded in Mark 9:14–32, Jesus heals a boy with an evil spirit. We are told that it "has robbed him of speech … it throws him to the ground … he foams at the mouth, gnashes his teeth and becomes rigid." It threw him into convulsions and often threw him into fire or water to kill him. Many commentators have described him as an "epileptic boy," and words like *murder, death,* or *suicide* come readily to mind, but Jesus commanded a "deaf and mute spirit" to come out. The identity of this demon was not obvious from the boy's actions, and this leads me to believe that Jesus discerned the identity of this evil spirit supernaturally rather than naturally.

Well over thirty years ago in the north of England, an incident hit the headlines: Three ministers tried to cast demons out of a non-Christian man and failed, whereupon the troubled person went out and committed a most gruesome murder.

Every Church of England diocese then formed its own deliverance group, which issued strict instructions to its diocesan clergy, and in some cases this meant that very little if any deliverance took place. Thus Satan won a very great victory over the churches in Britain and stopped a lot of Christians from doing what Jesus had commanded them to do.

Then this happened.

It was on a winter's night, when deep snow covered the Yorkshire earth, that I went "up north" to speak at a healing service. I was not aware at the time that although that murder had taken place in

Barnsley, the "failed ministry" had occurred *elsewhere,* and that I was now on my way to *elsewhere.* Neither was I aware that deliverance was now totally banned in the parish of St. *Elsewhere.*

I got lost, as I often do, trying to find the church on Saturday night, but I eventually plowed my way through the white drifts and arrived at my planned destination just in time. Despite the appalling conditions on the road, the place was packed with people and clergy from many miles around.

At the end of my talk I invited everyone present to stand, eyes closed, heads up, and hands held out while I prayed, "Come, Holy Spirit." The power of God came immediately, and that which had been hidden in darkness came into the light.

A man was thrown kicking and screaming onto the floor of the aisle near the front of the church, a lady yelled out in the upstairs gallery and crashed over, and another lady caused a scene toward the back of the church. The vicar leapt into action and marshaled his troops to the troubled spots, while I stayed at the front speaking into the microphone.

"Bless you, Lord," I said. "Thank you for all you are doing. Don't worry about the noise," I continued, addressing the congregation. "People are with them. Just let the Lord do with you whatever He wants to do."

We continued until it was time to have a closing prayer, and then they asked for my help. The vicar and his team were dealing with the man, but the curate and a woman who worked at the church asked me to help them with the lady downstairs.

"Come, Holy Spirit," I prayed, as I sat on a chair looking into the eyes of a troubled lady. Once I could see distress manifesting,

I spoke again. "Demon of Satan," I said firmly but without shouting, "I command you to come to the surface in Jesus' name." We then witnessed a change from distress to arrogance on her face, so I continued. "Demon of Satan," I said, "I command you in Jesus' name to tell me who you are." An affected, proud-sounding voice, not at all like the person in need, then spoke slowly, strongly, "Arrogance."

"Demon of arrogance," I instructed, "I command you to leave in Jesus' name."

Time after time the demons surfaced, named themselves, and then departed through the mouth as the lady coughed or retched into the tissues we provided.

"Right," I said after a while to the curate. "It's your turn."

"I've never done it before," he shared honestly.

"No problem," I said in an encouraging manner. "It's Jesus who does it in the power of the Holy Spirit and with the authority of God the Father. Just do what I did."

So the curate took my place and prayed, "Come, Holy Spirit." Instantaneously a smiling, sneering demon appeared on the lady's face, caused her to lean forward until she was eyeball to eyeball with the curate, and then said mockingly, "I see we have a beginner here."

"Ah yes," he responded quickly, "but Jesus is with me and He's done it before."

The demon snarled a little on the face of the lady at the mention of Jesus but didn't reply.

"In the name of Jesus," articulated the curate, "I command you to tell me what you are doing."

Slowly, with theatrical timing, the demon paused, looked straight into the curate's eyes, and said, "I'm making a monkey out of you."

"Tell me your name," demanded the curate a little more uncertainly.

The demon threw back the lady's head, laughed, and then in a high-pitched, demented voice sang these words to us: "Jeans, Jeans. Wrangler's Jeans. Levi's Jeans. Jeans. Jeans. My name's Jeans."

But "Jeans" wouldn't go, no matter how hard the curate tried. "I think I'd better have a go," I said with sadness in my voice, as I realized my attempt to teach someone else had failed.

We changed places and, as I looked once more into the lady's eyes, praying like mad, so to speak, the Spirit of God came upon me, and I knew the identity of the demon. "Your name is madness," I said, and the face of the entertainer was instantly replaced by the face of a miffed, angry demon who revealed its true colors. The unclean spirit left with no more trouble.

On Monday we cast another demon out of a lady back home and prayed for her five-year-old son who had a cancerous, inoperable tumor. He was completely healed. (The story can be read in my book *The Spirit Who Heals*.) Altogether, it was a significant few days for us.

The next day the vicar from St. *Elsewhere* phoned me. The man they had ministered to had not been able to get any help since the original incident, but the vicar had rung the bishop who now gave permission to recommence deliverance ministry in his parish. To God be all the glory!

Finding the Right Way to Minister

When Saul had an evil spirit, David ministered to him with music (1 Sam. 16:23); God used Peter's shadow (Acts 5:15) and Paul's handkerchiefs (Acts 19:12); Jesus initially resisted the approach of a Syro-Phoenician woman (Mark 7:24–30), took time questioning a boy's father (Mark 9:14–29), asked a demon its name (Mark 5:1–20), refused to let another demon speak (Mark 1:34), and drove out many spirits with a word (Matt. 8:16). The variety of ways for ministering to the demonized in Scripture point us once more to the need for discernment and listening to the Spirit of God.

When a certain grandma died, it was as though a bad smell seeped into the pores of every part of the fabric of the home. So the family moved, but the bad smell went with them. Grandma's daughter Elizabeth didn't know what to do, so, with her married daughter, Linda, she went searching for the answer.

Together they went to Birmingham Cathedral, to the spiritual home of the city, and there they met Canon David, who told them about Jesus and demons. He spent time getting to know them, shared the gospel with them, and in due course David prayed with Elizabeth to accept Jesus as her Lord and Savior. He cast out a few demons, and the odors left. The canon also left, moved to Oxford, and passed the family on to me.

Elizabeth and Linda joined a church, got into the Bible, prayer, and worship. The rest of their relatives also showed an interest. Elizabeth, despite having no real church connection, was very moral, and had very few "demonic" habits compared to most people today, and she was determined to put anything right we told her about. On one occasion she told us of twelve plates in their home with horoscope signs on them, each worth one hundred pounds. As we advised, they smashed all of their plates immediately—£1,200 worth.

Having made a commitment to Jesus, Elizabeth was puzzled that a troublesome demon would not leave, and it led us on a hunt for a long time. We did not know then about breaking soul ties and ancestral blood lines. Clearly Grandma had exerted a big demonic influence on this family, and now we needed to learn that it isn't just our own sins that can cause demonic problems, but the sins of our ancestors as well (Ex. 20:5–6).

On one occasion, as advised by some friends, we cut the blood lines while ministering to Elizabeth, and she felt pain in her navel area. Miles away—while in the bath—Linda simultaneously felt the pain and experienced bubbles coming to the surface of the water from her stomach region. Both of them felt sore for a week as if the umbilical cord had just been cut. In due course we were able to identify the demon that was causing the trouble as "antichrist," and it left.

After we ministered to Elizabeth, we spent time with Linda, because she had multiple sclerosis. Before she met us, she had one daughter, then suffered a miscarriage and was advised by the medical profession not to have any more children. In fact doctors told her it was likely she wouldn't be able to do so.

Friends then suggested acupuncture. After failing to bring any relief, the acupuncturist suggested spiritual healing, which eventually led her deeper and deeper into occult practices. Linda's condition deteriorated. Now that we knew her better, we began to discuss what Jesus had to offer her, and she asked us for help. We prayed for Linda's second child, carried out a funeral in church, and asked Jesus to welcome the little one who was made in the image of God into heaven. This led to Linda accepting Jesus as her Savior and Lord. We prayed for her to be filled with the Holy Spirit, and because of the family's history, made an appointment for Linda to do some deliverance with us.

We met in a room at the back of the church and prayed, "Come, Holy Spirit." Immediately Linda's teeth began to chatter, fear spread over her face and, from time to time, as she saw things in her mind, she began to scream very loudly. We pressed on, frequently praying words like, "Holy Spirit, help Linda to see Jesus. Help bring Jesus into the picture to sort out this problem."

The Spirit came and enabled her to see the demonic forces influencing the people who had offered to help her and the seriousness of what she had done. The whole incident took about three hours, with a break in the middle. What follows is a précis of Linda's own account of what she experienced.

> When we asked the Holy Spirit to come and minister to us, my teeth started to chatter, my body shook, and feelings of extreme terror poured into me, to an almost overwhelming level. Then in my mind I found myself in the room of a lady who was a "spiritual healer" that had been recommended to me. She came and stood behind me. I could see her hands running over my face while she was giving me spiritual healing, and as I glanced up at her, I knew why I was so frightened. She had the head of a demon and I was her prey.
>
> But fear turned to hope as the door opened, Jesus walked in, put out His arm and rebuked the spiritual healer. She cringed and slowly retreated

into the farthest corner of the room, spitting and hissing as her tongue flicked in and out like that of a reptile. Jesus took the position she had occupied, stood behind me, placed His hands gently over my face and eyes, took my hand and led me out of the room while He made long strokes with His hand, up and down and all around me. "I cut you off. I cut you off from this influence," He said. The terror lifted, a feeling of peace and soothing descended upon me and I felt my head resting on Him briefly.

The scene changed and in a few seconds mounting fear was clutching at my heart again as I saw myself in the room of another lady to whom I had been going for spiritual healing. Similar events ensued. Then another.

Next I saw the spiritualist church I had attended and the healers in their white coats who likewise were all demons, and I left with Jesus.

The scene changed once more as I saw myself at home with my companion. We were using a pendulum and there were two demons in the room, laughing at us and mocking. Jesus came in, told them to hop it and ordered all the demons out of the house, claiming it back for Himself. I saw my companion and myself go down on our knees and kiss His hands.

I felt very relieved, but I knew it was not over, for fear overwhelmed me again as I saw myself in the home of a clairvoyant I had visited. The atmosphere weighed me down as I sat at the table opposite a really vile demon. The door opened, Jesus walked straight over to the table, smashed His fist down in the middle of it, and said very aggressively, "This must stop!" He took me out of the room and severely reprimanded me, telling me never to do this again. I looked back at the room and the clairvoyant who was standing in the doorway feverishly trying to lure me back in.

More episodes followed, including my own thoughts of going into some kind of "spiritual healing" practice myself. Jesus walked through them all with me. As we left the last one, He told me that if I ever did anything like that again, far worse would befall me. He said I would be His disciple, proclaim the gospel and be obedient to Him, and then He walked away.

This decisive exit of Jesus indicated that the ministry for the day was over and that the episodes covered had been dealt with completely. It still amazes me to think that all we really did was to pray, "Come, Holy Spirit," and then sit with Linda for about three hours while Jesus revealed her sins, convicted her of them, and helped her to repent.

To complete the ministry, we borrowed the baptistery of our local Baptist church, and Elizabeth and Linda were immersed in a cleansing, dedicating ceremony. The Holy Spirit then spoke to Linda, quoting the angel Gabriel's words about the birth of Jesus and John, and one particular phrase stuck with her. "Nothing is impossible to God," the Spirit said to her (see Luke 1:37).

From then on Linda believed that God said she could have more children.

The medical profession was horrified that she was determined to have a go, but now, twenty years later, she has five. Linda has indeed continued to proclaim the gospel and has helped many others to know Jesus, and keeps well, although some of the symptoms of MS are still present.

Linda's sisters have all become Christians, as have their husbands. When Elizabeth's husband, Linda's father, Jack, rang me to tell me he wanted to become a Christian, he said to me: "I could not fail to become a believer, after all I have seen and heard."

One intelligent family dared to believe the Bible, investigated the evidence, saw Jesus as the answer, with signs following, and a whole family and group of friends have become Christians. Over the last twenty years, Jesus' prophetic words to Linda and the family have been fulfilled and stood the test of time. Today they all continue to spread the gospel of Christ.

8

SIGNS AND BLUNDERS

God spoke to me—as clear as a bell—while I was in the bath.

I was relaxing between the sessions of a four-day Christian conference at Brighton, looking forward to hearing Terry Virgo addressing us at the main evening meeting. A group from our church had made the trip together and managed to find an economical guesthouse near the conference center and seafront. I was not speaking, ministering, or in any way responsible for anything that was taking place, so I was taking it easy, learning a lot, and enjoying myself. It was absolute heaven—until God broke in.

"Tonight I want you to walk along the seafront," the Lord seemed to say. "There you'll see and recognize someone who is contemplating suicide. Engage them in conversation and give away your ticket for the meeting, where the person will be saved and restored."

It was only a thought. I couldn't really expect graffiti on the walls of the house, as happened with Daniel, or an angel to visit me, as one did Peter in prison, or a thunderous voice from above, as Jesus heard during His glorification, so I was content with just a thought in my head. But it was precise, it was meaningful, and it was urgent.

I attempted to put up some nominal resistance by asking myself a few questions. Was it better for me to hear my umpteenth talk at a conference or be instrumental in saving someone's life materially and eternally? *No contest.* Could I wait to test it with other Christians? *No, it might be too late if correct.* Was it against the teachings and commands of the Bible? *Definitely not.* Would it cause any harm if I was totally wrong? *Most unlikely.* My opposition was therefore minimal and I knew what I had to do.

I dressed and, without a word to anyone, left the guesthouse and stepped out onto the pavement beneath leaden skies and April showers. Soft, refreshing rain greeted me at first, but by the time I reached the English Channel, it had passed the heavy downpour stages and reached the torrential.

The seafront at Brighton is expansive: It features vast acres of roads and paths, boating ponds, paddling pools, and grassy areas with formal flower arrangements. Normally it is crowded, even in spring, with toddlers on tricycles, teenagers on skateboards, and the elderly in wheelchairs, but even mad dogs and Englishmen were not out in this.

Without an umbrella I trudged up and down for an hour or so with missionary zeal, as this was a serious word, and I took everything that the heavens threw at me, but there was not another soul to be seen anywhere. As time slipped by, the hotel lights came on and I knew the meeting at the conference center was well under way. I needed to find the person quickly before it was too late.

I prayed and prayed. "Lord, give me another word. Show me which direction to take. Lead me to the person in need," but the response was underwhelming. There were no more thoughts, no feeling of power or warmth, and no sense of God's presence at all.

And then at last I saw him—an Englishman with his dog, sheltering from the elements in a purpose-built hut. The Brighton Council was obviously familiar with weather such as this, and had prepared for all eventualities for those enjoying themselves beside the sea.

Excuse me ... I don't suppose ... were you possibly thinking of ... no, that wouldn't do. He looked happy enough anyway, as did his dog. I entered the haven in a more cautious and English way, trying to look nonchalantly like a fellow traveler in need of protection. "Turned out nice," I said, with a smile like George Formby. How was he? Fine. How was the dog? Fine. How was I? Soaked, miserable ... almost ready to jump off the pier? Not quite.

The rain eased as darkness descended and I made way to the conference center, where nobody bothered to check my badge, though I expect they would have kicked up more of a fuss if I had brought a dog onto the premises. Terry Virgo was coming to the end of his Gideon sermon, and the whole place was captivated.

"Marvelous, wasn't it?" said a friend in the foyer afterward, as I sought to restore myself with a cup of coffee. "Yes, particularly good last five minutes," I offered between sips. "You look a little wet, Peter," he commented.

I felt a little wet. But this is the reality. Sometimes we can get it wrong, yet better that than not try at all.

Prophetic Blunders

The character of prophecy in the Old Testament is one of absolute certainty and accuracy. In his book *The Gift of Prophecy*, Wayne

Grudem has some interesting headings when writing about this subject:

> The prophets are messengers of God....
> The prophet's words are words of God....
> To disbelieve or disobey a prophet's words is to disbelieve
> or disobey God....
> The words of a true prophet are beyond challenge or
> question.[1]

He entitles this particular chapter on the Old Testament "Speaking God's Very Words," supported by scriptural references. Perhaps the most telling one is Deuteronomy 18:20—"A prophet who presumes to speak in my name anything I have not commanded him to say ... must be put to death." I wonder how many people who leap up to prophesy in our charismatic churches might be restrained a little by that one.

The Holy Spirit was not given to all believers under the old covenant, but when God gave the gift of prophecy, those who spoke did so with unquestioned authority and accuracy. In contrast, when we turn to the New Testament, the certainty found under the old covenant is no longer there. Wayne Grudem writes this: "At first we might expect that New Testament prophets would be like the Old Testament prophets. But when we look through the New Testament itself this does not seem to be the case."[2]

Could it be that, despite the presence of the Holy Spirit who now lives inside every believer, the Old Testament prophets could hear God speaking more clearly than the New Testament prophets?

Could it mean that, although every Christian has received God's Spirit permanently within, we cannot now hear God as well as those who were anointed under the old covenant?

One day a lady and her daughter agreed to come with me to a meeting in Bristol, a trip of about two hours. She sat in the front of the car, her daughter sat in the back, and I asked her if she could have a look at our travel instructions. It turned out to be a very strange journey.

As we came out of the driveway, I immediately received definite guidance from my navigating passenger. We turned left, turned right, turned left, turned right—went all over the place instead of taking the main road to Bristol that I knew quite well, and she seemed to find different ways I had never been before in my life. After about an hour we didn't seem to be as far along the road as I expected we would be, but eventually I spotted a sign pointing to Bristol, "That seems to be the way," I said, and took it.

Without any more ado we headed toward Bristol, and as we came toward the outskirts of the city, I asked if my guide could get me there now. "Turn right," she said, definitely. "Turn left, turn right, go this way, go that way, go the other way, do this, do that, do the other, there's a church. That'll be it," she said. But it wasn't.

I stopped at the end of the road. "It's not the right name," I said. "It's not the right area. It's not the right place." Reluctantly she had to agree that it wasn't. "What have you been doing?" I asked.

"I don't do driving with maps," she replied. "I just do whatever the Lord tells me to do. So when you asked me to guide you to Bristol, I asked the Lord 'right or left?' And then when we got to Bristol, I just said to the Lord 'this way or that way?' and listened to whatever He said."

Perhaps God was having a bad day. I looked at the instructions and plotted my way with the map and eventually arrived at the right place about ten minutes before the meeting was due to start.

Our charismatic navigator was obviously working on the assumption that, since the Spirit lives inside every born-again Christian, we can all hear God as well as Moses did, even if it does add forty years to our journeys.

Blunders in the New Testament
John the Baptist

John appears to mark the end of Old Testament prophecy and the beginning of the New Testament era. "There is no one greater than John," said Jesus (Luke 7:28). He was the last prophet under the old covenant, and he was "filled with the Holy Spirit even from birth" (Luke 1:15). When he delivered his prophecies and Jesus appeared he said, "He must become greater; I must become less" (John 3:30).

This appeared to take place at Jesus' anointing. Not only did John's imprisonment curtail his ministry, but his authority and accuracy also waned. "Are you the one who was to come?" he asked Jesus, "or should we expect someone else?" (Luke 7:19). This means we can classify John as our first "signs and blunders prophet."

Peter

Peter heard God speaking to him. In Matthew 16:16, Simon Peter said to Jesus, "You are the Christ, the Son of the living God." Peter was right. Peter heard a message from God correctly. "Jesus replied, 'Blessed are you, Simon son of Jonah, for this was not revealed to you by man, but by my Father in heaven'" (Matt. 16:17).

Five verses later, however, after hearing Jesus' prediction of His death, "Peter took him aside and began to rebuke him. 'Never, Lord!' he said, 'This shall never happen to you!'" (Matt. 16:22). This time Peter thought he was right, but he wasn't. This thought did not come from God. "Jesus turned and said to Peter, 'Get behind me, Satan! You are a stumbling block to me; you do not have in mind the things of God, but the things of men!'" (Matt. 16:23).

If Peter could be led astray by the enemy, we can be too. (Matthew 4:1–11 shows that even Jesus could hear Satan speaking to Him.)

If ever there was a man who epitomized signs and blunders ministry, it was Peter. Jesus gave Peter power, authority, and an anointing from God in Luke 9:1, after which he declared both God's truth and Satan's lies, walked on the water and sank, drew his sword bravely, and then denied his Lord. He was one of the leaders of the New Testament church.

After the resurrection Peter "received the Holy Spirit" permanently (see John 20:22), but the blunders continued. One day Peter had a vision. "A voice told him, 'Get up, Peter. Kill and eat'" (Acts 10:13), but Peter got it wrong again.

"Surely not, Lord!" replied Peter (Acts 10:14).

In the Epistles, Paul recorded an incident that also involved Peter. "I opposed him to his face, because he was clearly in the wrong," wrote Paul (Gal. 2:11).

In Caesarea Philippi, Joppa, and Antioch, we find a New Testament leader getting it wrong. We see God using Peter in remarkable, prophetic ways in the Gospels, Acts, and in the Epistles, but he still made mistakes.

Agabus

"A prophet named Agabus" brought a word to Paul (Acts 21:10). Agabus was anointed, had received the Holy Spirit, and exercised a powerful prophetic ministry, but strictly speaking, his prophetic utterances contained inaccuracies: "The Holy Spirit says, 'In this way the Jews of Jerusalem will bind the owner of this belt and will hand him over to the Gentiles'" (Acts 21:10–11). The fulfillment of this prophecy is recorded at the end of the same chapter. But as things turned out, the Jews didn't so much "hand over" Paul to the Romans as try to kill him, and it was the Romans, not the Jews, who bound him (Acts 21:30–36).

This was a New Testament prophet who made two small errors. Paul still ended up bound and imprisoned as a result of going to Jerusalem, but the inaccurate details caused Agabus to fail the Old Testament test that the prophet's words are the very words of God. Here we have a third "signs and blunders prophet."

Government Structures of the Early Church

While there may have been a few inaccurate statements from the prophets in the New Testament, such as Peter and Agabus, after searching the Scriptures, I concluded that the main reason to believe there is less certainty under the new covenant is the way the early church set up its government structures. Once the community of the Spirit recognized that the Holy Spirit was poured out on all believers, they appointed leaders and elders and made decisions through joint prayer meetings, discussions, and councils, not infallible individuals. No longer did leaders like Moses or Samuel tell the people of God what to do, but the body of Christ listened to one another and to the

Spirit. It became a case of "it seemed good to the Holy Spirit and to us" (Acts 15:28). Acts and the Epistles suggest that the early believers prepared for failures when trying to hear from God.

In some ways Peter was like the Moses or Samuel of the early church, but when God sent him to the Gentiles with the gospel, visions, and signs, he was answerable to the eldership (Acts 11) and to the council of Jerusalem (Acts 15) for his actions.

Similarly, when the church of Antioch sent Paul out, he, too, was required to report to the leaders. James chaired the meeting, and he announced the fellowship's decisions (Acts 15).

The teaching in the Epistles, which continued from Acts, established the form of church government. It was based upon all Christians being able to hear from God, meeting together for prayer, using spiritual gifts, and gathering for discussions. John Stott wrote in his commentary on Acts, "There is no New Testament warrant for the one-man-band or a hierarchical or pyramidical structure in the local church."[3]

Here are some significant verses suggesting the New Testament does not assume the Old Testament certainty regarding words from God:

> Be transformed by the renewing of your mind.
> Then you will be able to test and approve what
> God's will is—his good, pleasing and perfect will.
> (Rom. 12:2)

> Now we see but a poor reflection as in a mirror.
> (1 Cor. 13:12)

Two or three prophets should speak, and the others should weigh carefully what is said. (1 Cor. 14:29)

Do not put out the Spirit's fire; do not treat prophecies with contempt. Test everything. (1 Thess. 5:19–21)

Train yourselves to distinguish good from evil. (see Heb. 5:14)

Test the spirits to see whether they are from God. (1 John 4:1)

In the New Testament we see examples of leaders and prophets making mistakes; teaching in the Epistles suggests prophetic errors will occur and that everything needs to be "tested." There are, of course, many examples of accurate words from the Spirit, but what we do not have under the new covenant is any assurance of infallibility. Rather, the believers "criticized" Peter (Acts 11) and reached conclusions "after much discussion" (Acts 15). We are likewise encouraged to "weigh" (1 Cor. 14) and to "test everything" (1 Thess. 5) because we "prophesy in part" and "see but a poor reflection as in a mirror" (1 Cor. 13).

Consequently I believe it is vital that we develop appropriate language for giving words that may be from God. Phrases such as "I believe God may be saying" or "I offer this thought, which might be from God" or "Would I be right in thinking?" or "Forgive me if I'm wrong, but I thought God might be nudging me into asking you …"

Such language gives other Christians the opportunity to weigh, control, and test the offered words. The responsibility passes from the individual to the body of Christ; others can then prayerfully verify what the individual has said. If we humbly and in love offer what we think God may have said to us, wrong words need not be damaging or disastrous.

The Bible gives examples and teaching about giving words from God to individuals (2 Sam. 12:7; John 1:47; 4:17–18; Acts 5:9); to small groups (Matt. 26:21; Luke 22:19–20; Mark 14:27; John 13:38); to churches (1 Cor. 14); and to larger gatherings (Mark 5:30; Luke 8:45). Once we have begun to receive and recognize communications from God, we can expect similar opportunities to come our way. We also need to allow for mistakes at every level.

On one occasion I thought God was giving me a message for an individual concerning "bondages" in her life. I never found out if I was right. I should have used the word *problems*. The concept of "bondages" had so many evil connotations in her mind that I was not allowed to give the rest of the communication. A "word of wisdom" is often needed to help us in giving a "word of knowledge" (1 Cor. 12:8 NKJV). I had wrongly assumed that if the word was from God, it would automatically be well received, no matter how I gave it.

At another time I gave two words concerning bodily complaints in a small group of five, neither of which was claimed. I was completely wrong. But afterward, as a result of my taking a risk and failing, two individuals sought me out for ministry. Both found it helpful, and one testified to it being an amazing event; she had never let anyone minister to her before and God came in great power. The words were wrong, but the moment appeared to be right, and God used it for His glory.

During a church service in Vancouver, I asked if there was a lady present called Doreen with a bad throat. No one claimed it. Then someone said her friend had a relative called Doreen, she had a bad throat, and would that do? We prayed for her publicly with no apparent success. I realized afterward I was wrong in doing this; at the time I was not prepared to accept failure graciously.

At a large gathering of several thousand in Harrogate, I heard John Wimber give a word for Mark and Alice. Time went by and no one claimed it. Eventually one of John's colleagues suggested it was meant for two friends called Mark and Alex. They were found later, and everything else in the message fitted them. I was greatly encouraged to see how others more experienced than myself were not always 100 percent accurate.

The Holy Spirit resides in all Christians, and we can all hear God speaking to us from the least to the greatest, individually and collectively; but in the New Testament, the words from God do not always seem as certain as those in the Old Testament. If Peter, Agabus, and Paul needed to be answerable to the eldership in the early church, I suggest we need the same sort of accountability. Road maps and satellite navigation devices may still be needed to help us find the way.

Moving On

In October 1992 my wife, Carol, was having her quiet time with the Lord when she sensed He was saying that 1993 would be the time to move. We had been at Christ Church in Birmingham since 1979, so this was not totally unexpected. I asked God about it in my own prayer time and He seemed to say, "Yes, but you are not to look for a job, read the advertisements, or begin applying for every vacancy you see. One will come to you by Easter Day."

Moving jobs, home, and church is not a small matter. Many thoughts that I thought were from God had never come to pass, so I asked hesitantly, "How will I know this is true?"

"You will have a brand-new car by the end of the year," God seemed to say, "and when the job appears, you will recognize it as right for you. It will meet all of your heart's desires."

Suddenly, after God's revelation to us in the autumn of 1992, we heard that my mother had seen a bungalow she liked and was thinking of moving after living on her own for fifteen years. Downsizing meant that she would be able to help us buy a new car—even though it didn't happen until January.

So with anticipation we prayed and waited for a job to arrive on the day we celebrated Jesus' rising from the dead. When all the services were over, we leapt up when the phone rang with expectation in our hearts. The Outer Hebrides perhaps, or the Scilly Isles, or the beautiful island of Jersey, where I became a Christian? No, it was someone wanting to make arrangements for a wedding. On Easter Day!

We went to Spring Harvest with some members of our church and had a great time—there's nothing like close fellowship in a holiday cabin—and then we returned home. I was out when the phone call came from a gentleman who used to accompany David Watson on his evangelistic meetings. *Must be getting on a bit now,* I thought to myself. "Would we be interested in a job near Wimborne not far from Poole Harbour?" he asked. I rang him back.

"Why didn't you ring before Easter?" I asked abruptly.

"Pardon?" he said in a posh accent.

"God told us you'd ring before Easter," I explained clearly to him.

"Oh, er … yes. Well, we hesitated a bit. We weren't absolutely sure," he bumbled.

"I'd have said yes, before Easter," I continued.

Anyway, he came to see us to talk about it. The fellowship in Dorset had prayed a lot, and one person had even received the word "Peter," with an unusual middle name beginning with *H*. (My middle name is Halliday.)

We met the churchwardens, who wanted us; the outgoing team vicar thought it was right for us; and the team rector wondered if we could start in September. We saw others from the Lantern Church who were lovely Christians, and we returned home on cloud nine.

That weekend my wife, Carol, went with our youngest daughter to visit her parents in Spain, leaving me to look after Amanda and Heather for two weeks. On Sunday night, the team rector from Canford Magna phoned me. Some members of the Lantern Church were not sure I was the right person for the job. Would I mind being included on a short list of four to be formally interviewed in a month's time?

I was devastated. I had never been interviewed for a job in my life, and Carol and I could not easily console each other on the phone. We suffered apart. The loopholes in our guidance were the small errors: Mum's car had not arrived by the end of the year; and the job had not appeared by Easter Day. But was it like Peter's and Agabus's errors, or would it turn out to be like my soaking in Brighton?

The next day I played cricket for the diocese and was out second ball for naught. This was bad news and good news. John Hughes counseled me all day in the pavilion, and he was terrific. He knew the situation at the Lantern, he knew me, and knew the Lord. His advice was very simple. "This is a spiritual battle," he said. "Encourage as many people as possible to begin praying immediately." He then listened to my moans and groans all day, still remained positive, and his love and advice helped me back to a more even keel, from which I could address the problem of the two errors. No matter how I felt, I needed to ask if it really was the Holy Spirit who was speaking to us.

I took my cricketing colleague's advice. Friends dotted about the country began praying for us, and some dear saints at Christ Church also joined in the battle, despite their not wanting us to leave. I asked a senior clergyman in Birmingham to pray for us, even though he told me his son was on the short list for the same job, and graciously he, too, prayed.

The fellowship at the Lantern and the other churches in the same team ministry prayed together and alone. One of the members of the leadership team, a key person, who was initially not sure I was the right person for the job, went down to the sea to be alone with God. The power of God came upon him, visited him in a vision, turned him right round, and he knew immediately that I was the one who should come.

God went before us, and I was eventually offered the post. Carol and I believed God guided us to Canford; some of the words that came to us from God were very special, but we still needed our discussions, prayers, weighings, and testings—not to mention the pain—before we were able to decide definitely that God had spoken.

Staying Put

We arrived in August prior to starting the new school terms, and I was installed as the team vicar of the Lantern Church in October 1993. When I was appointed, I was told there had never been a clergyman who had stayed more than four years.

In the following January, I spent a week with friends who had an anointed prophetic ministry and during that time they prophesied over me. One friend said he thought I might not stay at the Lantern as the team vicar for longer than three years, that the Lord had something else for me, and I would be moving on like my predecessors.

I found it very helpful when a respected prophet gave me a word, and I weighed it carefully. At the very least it made me pray and think about what God wanted me to do. When I came home, I did an audit on the whole area where we lived; there were seven thousand people, and I immediately noticed the roads were all named after airplanes.

We lived in Sopwith Crescent, and nearby was de Havilland Close, Hawker Crescent, Harrier Drive, and Cobham Road. Some people said it was because there had been an airfield nearby or that the flight refueling factory was in our vicinity. I also discovered the field that is now the residential area was a transit camp for German prisoners of war, and when they built the houses, they found items from a Luftwaffe (German air force) uniform.

After a while I realized the residents also had something of a transit-camp mentality, and many in the area did not stay more than eighteen months. Similarly, our church had become something of a meeting place that attracted people from ten miles around. Although these people experienced some wonderful worship and preaching, the church did not predominantly serve the area. We had a wide-open front door, a wide-open back door, and good numbers of "cruisematics" who drifted in and out.

I prayed very hard about this and felt the Lord say to me that the evil spiritual forces attacking the church and keeping us from what God wanted us to become were dominated by a ruling spirit called "Wanderlust." The enemy's strategy was to keep us moving on, to prevent the population and the church from settling, and therefore I made a decision to dig my heels in and to reach the people in our neighborhood.

There were in fact many other biblical, charismatic worship places for people to attend nearer their homes, and it was a greater priority for me to reach the people of the neighborhood rather than set up a meeting place for others—particularly when our church buildings did not have much room. We did not have the facilities in our small building for people coming from a long distance, many of whom were already Christians and were effectively stopping people in the area from coming to know Jesus. The visitors crowded us out and the church was disliked by the locals.

I also did some reading and took advice on spiritual warfare.

Having done my research, I was ready for a challenge. In 1995 our Canford church hosted a conference of about three thousand delegates at the Bournemouth International Centre. During this time I received a prophecy to the effect that my time was not now, but that it would come.

Shortly afterward I was asked to apply for a key post in the charismatic-evangelical Anglican world.

Interestingly, the two prophecies I had received earlier were now both helpful to me in making my decision. They helped me think through the options and consequences. I do not believe it is right for individuals to tell others what to do; we should pray, weigh, test, take advice, and ask others to share words that may be from God—but make our own decisions.

In the end I did not apply, but the whole process of weighing both prophecies was invaluable. I believe God wanted me to stay put at the Lantern. (That wasn't all. I also realized the other candidates were of a higher caliber than I was!)

At that time in our church we were £30,000 in debt, and almost immediately giving went up. In a short while we had a healthy bank balance and within a few years completed extensions to our buildings and facilities, all paid for. The church numbers dropped a little, but some new church members moved into the area, and the population settled into a more stable community. Some who moved in reached out to the neighborhood, and some local people were converted.

The New Testament suggests we need to pray, discuss, weigh, and test together in order to find His will, to obey Christ that His kingdom may advance in the place He has put us.

An Adult Relationship with God

There may be less certitude in the New Testament than in the Old, but there is now opportunity for a more adult relationship with God based on Jesus' love for us. We can grow closer to God through trust, discussion, and love, and become more mature in our dealings with Him.

In the Old Testament, people could be very secure but often failed to grow, whereas in the New Testament we can move "from one degree of glory to another" (2 Cor. 3:18 ESV) as we move nearer to Jesus. It starts when we make Jesus our Savior and Lord, and then progresses. The way I see it, there are four layers to the relationship we now enjoy with Jesus through the power of the Spirit.

1. Servants: "So you also, when you have done everything you were told to do, should say, 'We are unworthy servants; we have only done our duty'" (Luke 17:10). We start as unworthy servants.

2. Friends: Jesus then makes us His friends. "You are my friends if you do what I command" (John 15:14).

3. Adult children: Gradually a family likeness begins to develop. We become adult children who inherit and become responsible. "How great is the love the Father has lavished on us, that we should be called children of God! And that is what we are!" (1 John 3:1). We become princes and princesses of the kingdom.

4. Bride: Eventually, perhaps not before heaven, we become the bride of Christ. "For the wedding of the Lamb has come, and his bride has made herself ready" (Rev. 19:7). The day has arrived, and the betrothed is now the bride.

This is totally different from what was available in the Old Testament. To be in an adult relationship with God, we need to hear

Him speak, to speak to Him, and to know Him. Even so, our aim is not to know more, to hear more words, or to become more certain in our faith—it is to *know Him*. I believe this is why the new covenant is less certain than the Old Testament—that we may become more responsible, more mature, and make ourselves ready to be the bride of Christ.

Life would be much easier without the blunders, and I understand that many of us crave total assurance. Sometimes the road is difficult. But on the way we get to know Jesus better. The Spirit who lives inside us does speak to us, but not always as a policeman or examiner. I suspect that knowing God, and loving Him as He loves us, is better for all of us than certitude.

9

TEST EVERYTHING

A friend invited me to speak at a new fellowship group with about sixty people present. It was an evening formatted very much like the Wimber conferences, with musical worship first, after which I was scheduled to speak and do a time of ministry. Out of the blue, while I was standing singing praises, an arctic storm hit me, and I found myself having to sit down—my body numbed by Siberian temperatures. After a while I spoke to God.

"Okay, Lord," I said, "it doesn't seem to have affected anyone else, so why am I turning into a snowman?"

"I want you to give a prophecy," He said. "For this new church."

I don't normally do prophecies for churches, as I am not a great prophet, and I had only ever once given a word for a congregation before. On the other hand, I was the man on the spot, and if Jesus wanted me to do it despite being frozen, I was willing to try.

"What do I say?" I asked.

The Holy Spirit moved upon me, burned off some of the early frost, and roughly speaking, told me to say the new fellowship was going to fall like a pack of cards.

Great, I thought, *that's really nice. They will love this.*

"It is all being taped," said God. "I want you to give My word, whether they hear it or not."

When the time came, I was still feeling shivery, but I found myself able to hang onto a few thoughts. They went something like this:

"I think the Lord may have a prophecy for you, and I am sorry to say the Lord is saying you are in for troubled times. What has started well isn't going to go on well, people will not stay, and it will be difficult for those of you who run the church. After something like six months there may only be six of you left, and those who meet together will think about closing down, but the Holy Spirit will come, He will build the fellowship, and it will be a blessing to many. The reason God is giving this word now is that the Lord in six months' time doesn't want you to close, that everything is going to be good eventually, but you need to know this beforehand."

The words *lead balloon* came to mind, albeit that the ministry that followed was well received. But it all occurred just as the Lord said. The numbers faded away and after six months there were only six of them left. They were thinking of closing, but they met together and prayed, recalled the prophecy, and found the recording. They listened to it, prayed again, believed the word was from God, and within another few weeks the fellowship grew and blossomed.

A word from the Lord can be very helpful to a church, but everything needs to be tested, as Paul wrote to the church in Thessalonica:

"Do not put out the Spirit's fire; do not treat prophecies with contempt. Test everything" (1 Thess. 5:19–21).

The Test of Scripture

John warns us against deceivers and gives us this test: "Anyone who runs ahead and does not continue in the teaching of Christ does not have God; whoever continues in the teaching has both the Father and the Son" (2 John 1:9). The teaching of Christ, as passed on or approved by those who knew Him, has unique authority and can help us to discern what is of God and what is not.

We live near the second largest harbor in the world, Poole, which is difficult to navigate during low tide. So the authorities put poles out to mark the shallow water and the sandbanks. If we avoid the shallow places, we can likewise discover the areas where we can sail safely, catch the wind, and enjoy the breezes of the Holy Spirit. The Bible helps us to identify the dangerous places.

I remember reading an article by the spiritualist Doris Stokes in a women's magazine my mother left lying around. Doris described several of her meetings in which she claimed spirits of the dead were giving her information. She then gave specific "words of knowledge" about people who had died, followed by words about their relatives present in the room. According to the article, all the details were later verified; invariably the so-called departed spirits said what a pleasant place they were in, what peace they had found, and told their loved ones not to worry any more about them. In the seventies and early eighties, Doris could pack 'em in all over the country, filling a venue like the Albert Hall every night for a week.

This is a very sinister counterfeit, but one that is easily exposed by Scripture. The Bible forbids us to contact the dead or have anything to do with mediums (Lev. 19:31; Deut. 18:10–12; 1 Chron. 10:13; 2 Chron. 33:6; Isa. 8:19; Gal. 5:19–21; 1 Tim. 4:1; Acts 13), and will not allow us to believe that everyone will be saved (Rev. 21:8). Clearly, if Satan can convince people that everyone who dies will be okay, there is limited value in the gospel of Christ. Because those who received a "word of knowledge" at Doris Stokes's meetings felt greatly assured their loved ones were happy, many people assumed it was good and even of God. This is why Scripture must always supply the foundation, and words of knowledge can only ever build on that. The Bible is our major source in discerning whether words in our minds are from God or not.

Our first and firmest pole is vital. Any word that contradicts the teaching of the Bible is not from God, while any word that is positively supported by Scripture is more likely to be from God.

Trial and Error

Deuteronomy 18:22 says, "If what a prophet proclaims in the name of the LORD does not take place or come true, that is a message the LORD has not spoken. That prophet has spoken presumptuously." This means any word claimed to be from the Holy Spirit should be substantially borne out by circumstances, even if sometimes we get a few of the details wrong. I call this the test of trial and error.

In the summer of 2007, I visited Spain with my friends Phil and Gill and took a service in the Ermita Church beneath the elephantine mountain in Javea. Beforehand, while praying, Phil felt the Holy

Spirit saying there would be a lady there with a clubfoot whom the Lord wanted to heal, so I mentioned this during the intercessions in the service. Afterward, while most people went out onto the patio for drinks, Gill noticed one lady who was still sitting in church and went to help her.

Jenny was very tearful that day because it was the anniversary of her mother's death, and she was very grateful to receive prayer. Then, as a result of the word I shared, she also mentioned she had a bad foot, though it was not a clubfoot, and received more ministry. Kindly Jenny wrote to me about her condition and what happened.

> I had suffered with my right foot for several years and found it painful to walk. I tended to walk on the outer edge of my foot which was almost at right angles to my direction of movement.

> In June 2004—I fell down the stairs and damaged my right foot. My 2nd toe turned in towards the large toe and I found it difficult to balance and kept tripping over my feet.

> Oct 2004—I fell again over my right foot—I went one way and it went another and my husband Kaye found me on the kitchen floor. This time I had a cut over the eye and by morning I was black and blue down the whole of the right hand side. The foot was once again swollen. After the rest of me recovered,

the toe was still not pointing in the right direction, and when walking my foot got completely in the way.

June 2005—I had an operation on the foot. The surgeon broke the toe in two places, cut through the tendon, and he also broke the big toe and trimmed the bone. This left me hobbling in a plaster boot for six months.

December 2005—After the boot was taken off, the foot was very swollen and walking was difficult. I was told that this would be OK after exercise which I did, but the operation was not a success. I found it very difficult walking and because of the strange stance I had to adopt, it affected my back.

On that day under the mountain, Gill prayed and the Spirit came upon Jenny.

In the same week I prayed for Jenny at another meeting—for the Holy Spirit to come on her again, and by the following week she was able to bend her toes. Within a couple of weeks she was able to spread her toes. Every day the Spirit kept coming on her, and after a while she was able to stand on tiptoe and wear normal shoes instead of her orthopedic ones. A high point for Jenny was when she discovered she could wear high-heeled shoes, which she had thought she would never be able to wear again because the foot did not bend and was larger than the good foot. It is now nearly normal; the second toe points a little toward the big toe, but the foot is normal size, bends, and Jenny can walk on mountain paths with no problems.

We did not get everything right, but the test of trial and error (giving the word, finding some errors, but noting that it was substantially borne out by circumstances) enabled us to test that which was of God and to give glory to Him.

Asking the Right Questions

Before our church members offer prophetic words in our services, we like them to be sure of a few biblical principles. Here they are—all thirteen of them.

1. Are you a Christian?
2. Are you sure you are a Christian?
3. Have you received the Holy Spirit?
4. Are you sure you have received the Holy Spirit?
5. What makes you sure you are a Christian and have received the Holy Spirit?
6. Are you worshipping regularly with other Christians, reading your Bible daily, and praying for others to be saved, healed, and set free?
7. Does the word you are about to offer contradict Scripture?
8. Does Scripture support this kind of word?

Although this is the most vital test, it is one new Christians may not be able to apply for themselves. Consequently it is helpful, when a new Christian receives a word, if it can be checked with a leader.

9. Is this word necessary or will common sense do?

On one occasion I finished a funeral at the crematorium and suddenly realized I was near a maternity hospital where two of my parishioners had just produced offspring. "Will they be there, Lord, or have they gone home?" I asked. I felt very strongly the Lord saying, "I will not normally give you a 'word of knowledge' you can find out another way. You should have phoned before coming out." I took a chance and found one had gone home and the other was still there, but I remembered the lesson. I do not believe God ever intends to do our thinking for us. The supernatural adds to the natural rather than replacing it.

10. What damage will be done if the word is wrong?

Again this needs to be checked with a leader.

11. Is it a well-worn path or a change in direction?

If a word is the sort of thing you often say to others in your own name, then be a little cautious. If you have given several words of this type before that have been claimed and proved helpful, then go ahead—Jeremiah said the same thing again and again. If not, or it is your first word, then it may be worth checking with a leader before giving it, as it may be from your own subconscious rather than the Spirit of God. Instinctively, most of us feel a word is more likely to be authentic when it is not the sort of thing a particular person would normally say.

12. What good might be done if it is right?

As well as asking if this word is likely to advance the kingdom of God, I think we also need to look at how specific it is. I have come across people giving words like "a pain in the back" to large gatherings. It may be right to ask, "Have I enough details to identify one person in this meeting?" The larger the meeting, the more details we would expect a word from God to contain.

13. Is it good practice to give this word?

When we seek to give words with sensitivity, love, and humility, as Jesus did, we are likely to accomplish God's purposes, and it does not always even matter if we are mistaken in the details.

The Value of Sensitivity

There have been blunt, none-too-polite Christians in the history of the church who have given words from God with direct, challenging certainty and been greatly used by the Lord. This can be acceptable in some instances, providing the person is always right—we can never afford to be both rude and wrong. But I am not convinced the teachings of 1 Corinthians 13 or the example of Jesus ever justify a lack of love. Insensitivity does not appear to have been Jesus' own style when confronting individuals alone.

In John 4, Jesus begins an encounter with a Samaritan woman that within the culture of His day was rather risky and "ill-advised." It was an act of love, making Himself exceedingly vulnerable and open to misunderstanding. He asked the woman for a drink of water, and in this request she immediately recognized Jesus' acceptance of her: "You are a Jew and I am a Samaritan woman. How can you ask me for a drink?"(John 4:9).

This opened the way for Jesus to proclaim Himself the "living water." We cannot be sure if Jesus had information about the woman before the conversation began, or whether it was revealed to Him as they began to talk, but the way He addressed her is most illuminating: "He told her, 'Go, call your husband and come back'" (John 4:16).

Within her culture it would have been natural to assume she was married. Jesus appeared to know she was not married, but still asked her to call her husband. This was both wise and loving. If Jesus had asked, "Are you married?" the response could well have been, "How dare you!" followed by a slap across the face. But Jesus' request observed the etiquette of the day and also gave the Samaritan woman an opportunity to be honest, which she took. The question and subsequent answer achieved three things:

A. Jesus' loving, correct approach prevented the woman from becoming defensive or aggressive.

B. Her answer revealed that she was open to truth— I am sure some people in her position would have lied at this point.

C. Her answer also demonstrated that the suspected word from God or supernatural knowledge was correct. Jesus Himself may not have needed this confirmation, but lesser mortals like me often find such early affirmation to be faith-building.

In this example we can learn some principles for lovingly giving suspected words from God to individuals. A polite request led to an open and honest response and a confirmation of the word. This enabled Jesus to share the full extent of His knowledge: "You have had five husbands, and the man you now have is not your husband" (John 4:18). This accurate word then led many to become believers (v. 39). Jesus did not rush in with His word, but led up to it with courtesy and wisdom. His sharing of the gospel later proved decisive, as the word confirmed the prophet and His message.

If Jesus was sensitive in giving a word He inevitably found to be right, how much more should we do the same with words that may not prove to be so accurate? I believe that if we learn to be loving in the way we give words from God, we don't always have to be right.

In our church we sometimes have a time of worship when members of the congregation can approach a leader with a word prior to giving it. I do not, however, allow people to share prophecies for individuals in front of a congregation before those prophecies have been tested. Even if it is a "nice word," it can do damage, and the kingdom of God may not be advanced. I believe we are not being scriptural, loving, or responsible with the truth if we give words publicly before the individual concerned hears them. I am much happier giving a word to an individual afterward, preferably in the presence of a leader, and if possible recorded. If the word is helpful, it can later be shared publicly, giving glory to God. Words for healing are fine, particularly if ministry is available. It is helpful to think through how to test what people have suggested may be from God, but we also need to test the fruit of the Spirit: "By their fruit you will recognize them" (Matt. 7:16).

The Test of Ongoing Growth

Nothing compares to the joy of seeing people grow more like Jesus every day, no matter what age they are. Sue discovered the power of the Holy Spirit when He came to her and she experienced some of His "signs," but even though they caught her attention, what He did through her was even more special.

Sue, aged seventy-five, sat in her wheelchair at the back of one of our conferences, and everyone noticed how powerfully the Holy Spirit came upon her during all three sessions. In 2003 she had received two knee replacements, but the right one was not a success. Consequently her right foot stuck out at an angle, and though she could stand with the aid of sticks, Sue found walking a problem and needed a wheelchair.

As the Spirit moved powerfully on her during the third session, Phil and Gill moved in. Gill experienced considerable heat; turbulence spread throughout Sue's body, her whole leg began to shake, her right foot gyrated, and one or two people thought they heard a click as the right foot, unaided by human hand, turned round and pointed forward.

Since then I have received over twenty communications from Sue. Here are a few comments for you to enjoy.

> October 15: I'm the lady who sat in the wheelchair at the back of the church. My right foot still points forward and is no longer at an angle. I could stand up for the hymns in church this morning—no sticks going up for communion. Later this afternoon we went for about a mile walk along the canal and back, slowly, using my sticks.

October 23: The blessings continue. Yesterday was my third day not using the wheelchair. (I've been using a wheelchair since 1998.) I'm getting more upright. I walked to town. Walked to church. Up the tower to ring the bells. Was able to happily stand up for nearly the entire service—to raise my arms and sing praises. Chris [the vicar] asked me to come up and say a word which I happily did. "Let's give God a clap" said Chris, which we all heartily did. I continue to pray "Come, Holy Spirit" every day.

October 24: Dear Peter, I've just discovered that I matter to God. Words are superfluous! [All she wrote.]

November 4: I just keep praising God. Telling everyone.

November 18: Went to "swim mobility." Found I could kick my legs. Did ten lengths.

December 14: I'm tickled pink by the fact that the Holy Spirit is a person. I will see Christmas differently this year.

July 30: My foot that went straight at your healing service is still straight. Praise God!

The changes in Sue, not just physically but spiritually, continue to be a sparkling testimony to the fruit of the Spirit growing in her—a clear indication of a work of God in progress.

Prophetic Guidelines for Leaders

Here are some guidelines I suggest for leaders to ensure the validity of words and minimize possibility for harm:

- The content of the word must not contradict Scripture.
- The character and lifestyle of the person giving the word must be tested against Scripture (1 John 4:8).
- A person whose previous words from God have proved right is always worth a hearing (2 Chron. 18).
- People whose previous words from God have proved right may be valuable in testing someone else's word (1 Cor. 14:32).
- Consensus is worth noting, since all Christians have the Holy Spirit in them (Acts 15:25).
- A word confirmed by signs and wonders is a powerful word (Acts 11:11–18), *if* it fulfills the other criteria—not least, being in line with Scripture.
- A word that a person finds difficult to give or goes against what they normally say is a useful pointer to authenticity (Acts 10:14).
- If spontaneous words are allowed in a service, then a strong biblical leader needs to monitor everything and be prepared to break in if

necessary. All prophets are subject to the authority of the leaders.

- Words that are not controversial can normally be received at the time given, and be turned into a prayer. Words that are controversial or that may require action need to be tested by the eldership afterward.

- We normally meet to pray before a service. This is the time when we get most of our words as we ask the Holy Spirit to come, and we share them at the start of the service. During communion or after the service, we often invite people to come into the side-chapel for prayer. We record and share what the Lord has done.

- A word in harmony with Scripture from a proven prophet of good character—with signs and wonders following—is as good as we are likely to get until we can verify it experientially. The key principle is whether or not it advances the kingdom of God and bears fruit.

Here is an example of how a group of us eventually decided to give a word that we felt might be of the Lord, although there was doubt among us.

I used to belong to the East Birmingham Renewal group, which acts as a support and fellowship group for Roger Jones in his Christian Music Ministries. One Thursday night about fifteen of us gathered in the vicarage to pray before two performances of Roger's Christmas

musical, *While Shepherds Watched,* due to be held in the Birmingham
Town Hall. It was our policy to offer ministry at the end of a performance; over the years there had been some notable decisions for
Christ, and other healings and blessings have occurred. These two
performances were scheduled for the afternoon and evening on the
Saturday before Christmas, and we were praying specifically about
the form of ministry to follow each one.

As God's Spirit came among us, I sensed a word forming in my
mind and in due course shared it with the group. I felt God saying
we should invite all the children in the audience to go with the
members of the cast into the bar after the performance. (The bar
is not open for drinks when we book the town hall, but provides a
large, separate area where the choir often meets for prayer before a
production.) The cast could sing songs in costume and share something of Jesus with the children while we ministered to the adults
as the Lord led us.

Some practical problems surfaced, but there was a general consensus that this was a good idea and might even be a "God idea."
Unfortunately, Roger was unable to be present that evening, so he
didn't receive the message until Friday. Word came back to me that
Roger was not very keen on the plan, so I simply left it. Having
shared what I thought God might be saying, the responsibility was
no longer mine.

On Saturday morning I drove Roger, with members of the cast
and the costumes, in our minibus to the town hall. On the way Roger
told me he was unhappy with my word, which others had conveyed
to him. Immediately I responded, "You must make the decision. It's
your musical, you're in authority. You know I've sometimes been

right and sometimes been wrong. See what you feel the Lord says to you as the morning goes by."

I believe God gives authority for specific situations and roles. I do not feel we have authority over another person except in such definable areas. When I was at St John's College, I was under the authority of our principal, Michael Green, while involved in all college activities. All, that is, except cricket: I was the cricket captain. Michael sometimes played for our college cricket team, and when we were on the field of play, he came under my authority when, I'm delighted to say, he did everything he was told. As the field of activity changed, so did the authority role.

When we are in church where I am the vicar, Roger comes under my authority. In the town hall, however, our roles were reversed: He was in authority; I gave a word, and Roger was left to weigh it and make the decision. He accepted his responsibility fully and agreed to think and pray about the word I'd given.

As the large choir prayed before the rehearsal, Roger chose to share my word and people made encouraging prophetic noises. While the others were rehearsing, he asked me to check with the management to see if it was possible to use the bar, and they were very helpful and cooperative. Obviously if management had refused us permission, we would have had a negative but definite answer to our prayers.

Shortly before the performance Roger relaxed in his dressing room, and as he did so the Spirit came upon him and seemed to confirm the word in his own mind, so he acted upon it. The children loved it: Joseph and Mary and the shepherds and angels held their hands, took them to a side room, sang songs with them, and shared stories about Jesus. Roger asked God to come upon the adults, and one or two words about specific sins drew people to the ministry team afterward confidentially.

Roger had been able to weigh various elements: the word itself, the one who had given it, the sign of the management's cooperation, and his own inner conviction—all of which led to a blessing for young and old. In some ways his hesitation and testing made the eventual obedience and blessing so much more certain and helpful.

Heads or Tails?

In the Old Testament a priest would use the "urim and the thummim" to know the will of God. It is the equivalent of tossing a coin today. Gideon also laid out a fleece to discern God's will. Still uncertain, the following night Gideon asked for another sign.

> Gideon said to God, "If you will save Israel by my
> hand as you have promised ... make the fleece dry
> and the ground covered with dew." That night God
> did so. (Judg. 6:36–40)

Under the old covenant it was also common to cast lots. They cast the "pur" (the lot), which is where the Jewish festival "Purim" comes from. Peter also used lots before the Holy Spirit came on him on the day of Pentecost, though there is no evidence of him doing so afterward (Acts 1:26).

I am not happy with fleeces, lotteries, or the tossing of a coin. These were Old Testament practices, but in the New Testament all

believers have the Holy Spirit and can know the mind of Christ
(1 Cor. 2:16). This is the way prescribed after the day of Pentecost
for discovering the will of the Lord.

Worse than all, however, is the occult practice of "bibliomancy."
Some Christians use this practice of dipping into the Bible for
guidance—sometimes sold in Christian bookshops as lucky verses. If
you use the Bible like a pack of tarot cards, do not be surprised where
your guidance comes from—taking verses out of context is the way
Satan tried to tempt Jesus (Matt. 4:5–7).

In church we test everything against the Scriptures; we use the
test of trial and error, and the eldership "weigh" all words given in
every service. This is so we can clear space for God, put up our sails,
and allow the Holy Spirit to speak to us all of His presence, power,
and love. Consequently, when He comes, we are not surprised to
hear of the wonderful works of the Lord changing lives.

In 2007, I was speaking at a church where I was delighted to
meet Claire, one of the churchwardens. She kindly shared with me
how God came, spoke, and healed her in a service.

One day Claire met some Christians, attended church, and
experienced love from the fellowship. After a while she surrendered
to the Lord on her hands and knees at the foot of the cross, in an
empty church. This is her story:

> On the 19th August 1998 my GP told me that I
> had Metastic Malignant Melanoma resulting from
> medical negligence and missed diagnosis, leaving
> me untreated for four years. This resulted in the
> spread of the original mole to my lymph glands.

The following day I attended the Oncology department of a certain clinic, to be told after a few tests that I was not worth treating. I did not fit the criteria for this very toxic and nasty drug which cost £25,000 because of the spread of the cancer. He told me to go away and have a happy year. Fortunately the Royal Marsden [a specialist hospital] took me under their wing and gave me the treatment.

In 2001 the tumours spread to my lungs and, following a scan on the 31st March, I had a period of two months to wait before they rescanned me, to establish the speed of growth and spread of the tumours, in order to come up with the appropriate cocktail of chemotherapy. So, in the mean time I had to wait. It coincided with a planned visit of Doctor Roger Sapp from America to Christ Church.

It was a dear friend who suggested that I attend the teaching sessions and said I should go to the day-time teaching for clergy and leaders. The evening service was likely to be really busy.

I remember the day so clearly because I have never heard such an interesting, humble and gentle man preach so clearly and passionately about healing. I was totally absorbed by what he had to say about the entire issue. He spoke of our desire to be healed personally; did we really and truly want to be healed *now?* He spoke of the doubt that people have over healing which blocks the ability to be healed,

almost like clouds covering the sun and preventing
the sunlight from shining through.

And Claire heard it as if it was God speaking directly to her.

Later he invited people to come forward for healing
and I saw several clergy healed from back pain. He
then asked for anyone with a serious illness to come
forward. My friend tapped me on the back and said
very directly, "Go now, it's your turn." I remember
receiving the gift of faith while I was walking forward, knowing that at that very moment the Spirit
was going to heal me completely.

Dr. Sapp then asked very briefly what I wanted
healing for. I told him I had just had tests and I
had two tumours on my left lung following a recent
scan. I said that I was not having any treatment and
would have another scan in six weeks. He told me
to place my hand on the area. He asked for permission to place his hand on top which he did. He
then prayed in the name of Jesus [for me] to be
healed from the cancer. Within 30 seconds I had a
real burning sensation in my chest and I felt boiling
hot. My face went red with the heat and I felt a
real sense of peace and joy at the same time. I must
have stayed there for about 3–5 minutes while Dr.
Sapp continued to talk to everyone but remained
with his hand on mine. I was beaming with delight

and full of the Holy Spirit. He then turned to me and said, "Very clearly we are going to see a miracle here, Claire," and I replied, "I know." I left to collect my daughter from school shortly after that, and for at least half an hour my chest was still on fire.

Six weeks later I returned to the Royal Marsden to be rescanned and to have a chat with the Registrar and Chemo nurse. They discussed all the options of what they might give me when I received the results the following week. At the end I told them that I wouldn't be needing any treatment because I didn't have cancer anymore. I explained that I was a Christian and that I had had prayer and that I was totally healed from the cancer. They smiled and tried to understand by saying, "it is great to have something that gives you hope," but of course they didn't really believe me!

The following week I returned to the Marsden for my results.

As I sat in the clinic room for what felt like hours, but must have been only a few minutes, I was so excited knowing I was going to hear good news. The same doctor and chemo nurse came in holding my notes and politely shook my hand and sat down. The doctor just didn't know where to begin—he was almost speechless. He held in his hands a copy of the before and after scans and showed me one by one the evidence of the tumours

and then the second scan that said there was no
evidence of any cancer anywhere in my body. He
said that everyone was amazed and they had had
to hold a meeting to discuss it with all the team
to analyse the results. They couldn't make out how
this had happened. They were surprised by my calm
reaction and I just said I knew I had been healed
weeks ago and had got accustomed to the idea and
they had just confirmed what I already knew in
black and white.

They let me keep the results, which I have to
this day, with another copy given to Bruce Collins,
who was our Team Rector at the time.

When Claire believed God was on her case, took Roger's advice,
and cleared her mind and spirit to concentrate on Jesus the healer,
the Holy Spirit spoke in power, giving her the gifts of faith and healing. The simple formula for all New Testament healing is that we
"claim" what God "names." The key is knowing when God "names"
something—that is why we need the Spirit who speaks. The test of
time has shown that it was the Holy Spirit who was speaking to
Roger and Claire at Christ Church.

10

FACING THE END

Carol and I have lived in paradise by the River Stour in Dorset for four years. This is where John and Diana Collins resided when they pioneered the Alpha course in the rectory at Canford Magna before they moved to Holy Trinity Brompton in London and passed it on in embryo form to Nicky Gumbel, whom God used to make it the worldwide phenomenon it is today. Now we have a wonderful little hall under the trees with all the facilities, where groups can gather, dine, share ideas, and discuss the Christian faith together. Regularly some come to Jesus. It is a very popular place for Alpha meetings.

I was due to speak at the Holy Spirit Day during one of our courses. Before I started, one of the helpers was chatting with me, and as I tried to talk back to him, some of the words that came out of my mouth got strangled and didn't make any sense. I excused myself and prayed; my speech returned, and I was able to do the talks. But it was worrying. Maybe I was tired.

I invited those who so desired to make a commitment and had the great privilege of asking the Lord Jesus Christ to come into people's lives. The new believers had a go at speaking in tongues, and I asked the Holy Spirit to come on everybody. He came and all felt His power. One or two people had serious illnesses, and one person was in a wheelchair, so we laid hands on them. Though there were no great miracles, the Spirit of God was very tangible. At the very least I believe it was the beginning of a salvation event for some—maybe all.

The next day I had a little sleep in the afternoon before a clergyman came to visit me. We chatted in the lounge, but as we spoke, virtually everything I said to him turned into gobbledygook. He looked at me and realized that something was not right. "You talk and I'll listen," I said. "Talking doesn't seem to be working very well for me at present."

On the following Saturday I was due to speak at another Alpha course away day we were hosting in our little hall beside the river. There were about thirty people present, and I was to do all the talks. I rested on Friday, and after much prayer I managed to do the first talk.

Following the coffee break I carried off my second talk with my usual brand of quirky humor and stories, leaving nothing out, but by this time I was tired. Nevertheless I was pleased I had done two talks without scrambling my words, and enjoyed yet another excellent meal that materialized.

One of the ladies there had bought one of my books a few months before, knowing I was to be the speaker at their Alpha, and she asked if I would sign it. So I took the book and tried to write, "May the Lord bless you mightily in His Name," but I wrote, "Some had a bit …" The words I had written on her book made no sense.

Realizing I had ruined her book, I excused myself and took the book away. It was a long time before I could actually write what I wanted to write in another copy.

I looked at what I had first written with puzzlement, but somehow God and the prayers of the body of Christ helped me through the day.

Later that evening I had a go at my sermons, but found writing the talks proved to be a very similar experience to writing in the book. It took a long time to accomplish, but somehow on Sunday, I managed to preach three times.

On Monday we went for a break before Christmas to Spain, where Carol's mother lives. They asked me to speak at church, even though those who knew me well said I was not quite myself. I was supposed to be writing a book while on holiday (this one), but that was very difficult because my words were all jumbled, and every sentence took forever.

When I returned, I tried to do the early morning Sunday service in church, but erred and strayed miserably like a lost sheep. The congregation had to say the liturgy for me while I stood behind the table and had to make do with muttering a few words from time to time. At the main service I couldn't do the sermon, so Carol read it from the pulpit. Someone else had to do the evening service.

That's when I realized I was seriously ill. I went to the doctor but got an appointment to see the nurse. She said, "Oh you don't seem too bad to me," but later a doctor friend said, "That isn't good enough." So I spoke to my doctor the next day on the phone. He asked a few questions, and on Wednesday they took me to the hospital where they did a few tests. They thought I'd had a mild stroke.

Over the next three weeks I got worse and worse, until in the middle of the night Carol had to ring for an ambulance. I was taken into hospital where the doctor at Accident and Emergency realized it was a brain tumor.

I was admitted to hospital and finally the doctors came to see me. "We have carried out all the tests," they said, "and we don't really know quite yet what the situation is. It may be that we can remove the tumor and everything will be fine. It may be that we can't remove it and everything will not be fine. And it may be that we will do something in between." At this stage I did not know that there were different kinds of brain tumors from which some recovered very well, and some didn't.

On Friday morning, Andy Perry, the vicar from Poole, came to see me in the hospital with his curate Paul, and the Spirit came to me in a special way as they prayed for me. It was lovely just to be ministered to by others, and after they prayed, the specialist from Southampton spoke to me on the phone and said, "I'll do the operation and take it out for you."

It sounded to me as if I could now have the tumor removed and everything would be fine. So they booked me in for a New Year's Eve operation and in the meantime sent me home to enjoy Christmas with my family.

People were so kind—cards, flowers, messages, prayers, emails from everywhere, and the body of Christ rang from all over the country to say they were praying for me. I had spent a lot of time in the last two years traveling around the country to places like Aberdeen, Birmingham, London, and even Great Yarmouth, where I dropped a bit of a clanger when I first arrived there with one of my mistimed funnies. "This place looks like the end of the world," I commented when I saw the east coast; but they responded well. "Oh no," they said, "that's Lowestoft." But even they prayed for me.

For two years—since my last book came out—I had spent a lot of time speaking as well as running the church at Canford Magna, so cards, promises of prayer, and flowers now came from everywhere. When we are in need, the body of Christ is the most wonderful group of people on the planet. We had good times for two years, opening up the Bible together, ministering in the power of the Holy Spirit, and one or two people were healed, as I have shared in this book.

I had been really well too, had not suffered from any colds or flu or anything for two years, never needing to cancel any speaking engagements. It seemed as if the Lord helped me to do everything He wanted me to do. For two years I went on the road and God turned up every time; it was very special, He blessed many, and then suddenly all this love came back to me from those whom I had visited. Everyone loved me like never before, and I wept in joy every day as the cards, phone calls, and flowers broke me up. One Pentecostal Church of three hundred members stopped in the middle of their service on Sunday so they could pray for me.

My operation was scheduled for Monday, but the hospital rang during the weekend to say that there was no bed and no operating theater available for me. I was not totally surprised, knowing something about spiritual warfare and the National Health Service, but I knew the body of Christ would take it on in prayer for me with fervor. At first the hospital said there was no bed, and then on Sunday morning they rang me and said, "The situation has just changed. Somebody who had a bed and an operating theater booked has now moved away, and you can have their place." So I was taken to Southampton to prepare for the operation—I was to see one of the best specialists in the world.

Carol and the family came with me on Sunday, the day before the operation, and went home at 8:00 p.m. I spent the afternoon with the family, but at 9:00 p.m. the specialist came to see me, and the evening turned out to be a very difficult time for me. On the phone a week ago he had said, "I'll take it out for you," and I had got the idea, as had Carol and the family, that he would remove the brain tumor, and I would be fine. But now he said, "No, I'm afraid it doesn't look as though this is going to be that simple. We shan't know definitely until you have the operation, but I don't think we will be able to take it all away, and it may be the very worst kind. We'll do the operation because I think it will improve your situation, and it might help you a certain amount."

So after hearing that I was going to be fine, I was now going to have the operation and not going to be fine. I couldn't sign my consent forms because my brain was splattered, and the surgeon talked about getting Carol to come back to sign them for me. I looked at him and said, "How much do I have to sign?"

"You just need a signature there," he said. I prayed, picked up a pen, and scribbled.

"That will do," he said.

Strange though—when he had gone, the peace of God was still in that place. I was given my own room with a television and my own bathroom, the best that money could buy. I was about four floors up with a view over the city of Southampton. I just lay on the bed and prayed, sensing that everybody else who was praying was also taking part in what was taking place spiritually. I had a good night's sleep; I sensed the presence of the Spirit, and I felt fine. We didn't really know the situation, but Jesus was in control; I got a well-ventilated private room with a view, and I now seemed to be ready for the operation.

The next morning more complications arrived as the specialist could not do the operation. An emergency happened in the night; he needed to perform a seven-hour operation, and the theater that was booked for me was used for somebody else. The surgeon was not available, but people prayed.

Then suddenly an Indian man, a very experienced neurosurgeon who had been at Southampton for years, came to see me. "I've found another operating theater that isn't being used," he said. "I'll do it for you and we'll try and take it all away."

Oh, I thought. *He is going to have a go at taking it all away.* I rather liked the idea of being healed by the Indian subcontinent rather than the National Health Service. I prayed, and then five minutes before I was due to go into the operating theater, Carol arrived. We were able to say "hello" and "good-bye" and have a prayer. The night before, the specialist had reminded me that this was a serious operation; he was going to remove part of my brain and "not everybody recovers," but I felt at peace. I had a two-hour operation and time to recover, and then Carol was there with the children and I was all right, with time to spend with the family before they went home.

It was New Year's Eve. I had been married on New Year's Day, so the children reminded me of my wedding anniversary, but it was more special being with Carol and the girls knowing the operation was now over. For the first time since I was married, I had to see the New Year in without Carol, but God made it up to me.

At midnight I was wide awake, having been in the operating theater all afternoon, and as I looked out of the window, New Year's came, and the sky lit up for over half an hour with the most glorious firework showers from heaven I had ever seen in my life. Cascading fountains invaded my fourth floor through the window, and I took part in the praise that was now exploding all over the city. I could see everything from my room, and it seemed to me as if God was celebrating with me. It was emotional, very emotional, being with the presence of the Lord with the stars in the night sky, and I enjoyed myself believing the holy angels were playing in the emanating volcanoes and falling stars. God illuminated the clear sky in glorious iridescent colors, as if every shade of the covenant rainbow was there just for me, and the Lord felt very close.

I had a good night's sleep and was looked after in my own room with meticulous, loving care. The rest of the family came on my thirty-first wedding anniversary, so we had presents and spent the whole afternoon in my little room with cards all over the place, enjoying being together, and we had a party.

When the family left at about 8:00 p.m., I lay on the bed. This time the nurses finished and left me to my own devices. The Holy Spirit came powerfully into my room, and I had a vision of Jesus. It was more than a vision really, and I sensed a close encounter with Him as my spirit soared. In my mind's eye I saw the Pietà statue of Michelangelo from Rome, by the door of St. Peter's, which I think he carved out of marble when he was about twenty-four years old. It is a very moving sculpture, representing the body of Jesus being cradled and cared for by His mother Mary after He was taken down from the cross.

In my vision this beautiful work of art hovered over me as I lay on my bed, and it felt as if the body of Jesus was covering me. It spoke of what Jesus has done for me, and I wept like I had never wept before. There was the body of Christ, loving me, and I felt healed spiritually, eternally, and emotionally as the dam burst.

I was brought up in no-nonsense Yorkshire, and all my life I have been a performance-oriented person, driven by my father, whose own father died when he was seven. From an early age I felt compelled to succeed. Even when I became a Christian at the age of fourteen, everything was about doing, succeeding, achieving, trying to bring people to Jesus in my own strength. When I became a clergyman, I always wanted to be running the best church or preaching the best sermon or writing the best book. I put everything in the spiritual language of "doing it for Jesus," of course, but most of all I wanted not to fail. My life had often been one of tiredness, going from one thing to the other, one appointment to another, speaking, ministering, just trying to get through life. Trying to do what I thought was right, but haunted by the fear of failure and always wanting to succeed, for my dad, or for Jesus, or for me.

Now everything's changed.

When you are lying on a bed knowing that you may not have long to live and may never work again, but Jesus is there covering you—because He has died for you—nothing else matters. He has put me right with God and with people, and even now is putting me right with myself. I can't do anything now to save myself, but because of the vision, the presence of Jesus, and knowing what He has done for me, I feel washed, cleansed, and renewed.

It is the message of the Alpha course that Jesus has saved me, and all I have to say is yes to the gospel of Christ and put myself into His hands. As I'm writing this, I have been weeping every day, with joy. I have got in touch with my emotions for the first time in my life. And He is here, all the time.

Most of my life I have been looking for my emotions. Those who tried ministering to me—psychiatrists, psychologists, and counselors—thought they might have been hidden behind the sofa or in the garden shed, but I have now found them in Jesus. He has covered me and died for me, and I have been expressing tears of joy ever since that moment. I suddenly felt gloriously free.

Ten days later we got the verdict. There was nothing they could do. They were very sorry. Maybe a year.

There was, however, one further problem—the reaction of the body of Christ at my situation.

In 2006 when I published my book on Christian healing, explaining what I believe the New Testament teaches about the subject, I shared many stories of people being healed. For two years I traveled the country speaking at conferences and ministering in the power of the Holy Spirit, and now I have discovered that, medically speaking, I have a terminal brain tumor. This means I now must learn how to respond to all the love, care, prayers, and advice that has come to me. I receive responses from three basic groups of Christians:

1. Those Who Do Not Believe God Heals

The middle-broad church contingent has all been very supportive and very loving toward Carol and me. Bishops, archdeacons, deans of various kinds, and many other colleagues of other denominations have been so kind and promised to pray for me. But most of them do not believe in a God who does miracles, breaks in, or turns things around: If the medical profession says it is terminal, it is. How I wish they could meet Claire, the churchwarden from Christ Church Harrow, see her medical records, and encounter a real healing done by the Holy Spirit.

Without this experience they help in every way they can with their theology focusing on God helping us in our suffering in this life, much practical love, and the hope of heaven. Most of them seem not to have tasted a God who heals, speaks, or comes, believing in one who winds the universe up and lets it run like a clock. But I have been greatly loved by them all.

What they need is a word from the Lord.

2. Those Who Believe God's Will Is for Me to Be Healed

The extreme charismatics and Pentecostals take a different view and express it to me differently. The language they use is very much about claiming the victory, commanding the blessing, throwing out Satan, taking a stand on the "Word," quoting Scripture, and not taking no for an answer. Sometimes they are led of the Lord to tell me what I am doing wrong—for if I am not being healed, then in their eyes I am clearly doing something wrong. I am told to do more ministry, more casting out, to repent or listen to tapes or read books that have the answer. It is amazing how many of the extremists all seem to have specialist gurus with specialist answers, but it is also interesting how they all seem to offer different solutions—like Job's comforters, queuing at the door with their accusations.

They don't seem to take death seriously, as if they all expect to be transported to heaven at the end of their lives like Elijah. "Suddenly a chariot of fire and horses of fire appeared and separated the two of them and Elijah went up to heaven in a whirlwind" (2 Kings 2:11).

In my Bible he was only one of two who made it without the help of undertakers. It is interesting to see what happened to Elisha, who inherited a double portion "of Elijah's spirit" (see 2 Kings 2:9) and had a powerful healing ministry. God used him to heal Naaman from leprosy, restore the sight of a vast army, and raise the dead, but he did not go to heaven in a chariot: "Elisha was suffering from the illness from which he died" (2 Kings 13:14).

Elisha died from a sickness—even though he served God till the end (2 Kings 13:20).

In the past I always tried to correct poor biblical theology with good biblical theology. From my sickbed, however, I can see much more clearly, and it doesn't look like a theological problem at all— more to do with the lordship of Christ. The extremists appear to me as those who really believe they can tell God what to do. The answers are entirely in their hands, and I can hear them saying, "It's all about me. The power of heaven is available for me, to do whatever I want to do." It all feels wrong, so wrong. As if I can do it "my way."

What they need is a word from the Lord.

3. Those Who Believe God May or May Not Heal Me

The biggest group that has communicated with me, however, is the one that maintains God may or may not heal me. "God may heal you or He may not," they say, "but we are praying and believing that He will." The faithful members of Canford meet regularly to pray for me and have formed a prayer chain for which I am so grateful. God sends encouraging words at regular intervals, and the very least I can say is that everyone seems to want me to be healed—which is very kind. But not many have any firsthand experience of Jesus actually healing an inoperable tumor, like Claire's.

In my book *The Spirit Who Heals,* I told two stories Graham Cooke shared with me. One person was healed of a brain tumor, and one was told by the prophet that he was going to die. The second person then led a number of people to Christ before he died, and the other person was healed after much prayer. A positive result for both of them—knowing and hearing the voice of God is so helpful.

What this group needs is a word from the Lord.

Is There a Word from the Lord?

So at a time when I felt very close to God, I remembered that this is a book about "the Spirit who speaks," and I asked Him what He wanted to say to me. Is there a word from the Lord for me? God told Moses when he was going to die; He told Elijah when he was going to depart; and He told Jesus when He was going to be crucified. There is a time to die.

I believe the Spirit of God has told me that I will do everything He wants me to do, finish my race, and that will be sufficient for me. I believe that the night I saw the vision of the Pietà was the moment God not only came to me but spoke to me and told me I will not be physically healed.

I believe I may never do another Alpha course, but what a privilege it has been to see others come to know Jesus—His presence, His love, and the freedom He can give. I know all who have said yes to the Lord can look forward to spending the whole of eternity with Him. I am now worshipping God every moment of every day and praying for those who pray for me, that they will also enjoy God's peace and love always.

STUDY GUIDE

Chapter 1: The God Who Speaks

1. How would you respond to the following statement?

   I was unable to find anything in the New Testament to suggest the promises God made to the disciples and the early church are not meant for us as well. After the Spirit speaks on the day of Pentecost, Peter promises that the gift of the Holy Spirit is "for all" (Acts 2:39). When we see God face-to-face, then the spiritual gifts will cease, but the New Testament gives no indication of this occurring before then (1 Cor. 13:9–10).

2. Do you expect God to speak to you? If so, why?

3. How would you respond to someone who says that
    God speaks today only through Scripture?

4. How might we cultivate stillness, so that we can
    hear God speak? For example, what routines and
    disciplines might help? How might our prayer lives
    provide more space in which to hear God?

5. What are good motives for seeking to hear God?
    What are some wrong motives? What are some
    mixed motives we might have to work through as
    we listen to God and try to act on words we believe
    we have received?

6. Peter was disappointed when someone confided pri-
    vately that a word given publicly at a large meeting
    was meant for him. Would that have disappointed
    you? Why? How might you minimize such disap-
    pointment? For instance, would it help to address
    your desire to look good? Is this largely a matter of
    perseverance in finding the intended recipient of a
    word?

7. Peter says, "a present-day word from God may there-
    fore illustrate Scripture, help to apply Scripture,
    authenticate Scripture, and enable Christians to
    fulfill the commands of Scripture, but must always
    be tested by Scripture." Give some examples of

possible words God might give to help someone to apply or obey Scripture. (The examples in this chapter have focused on healing, but can you think of other areas of life?)

Chapter 2: Is There a Word from the Lord?

1. Why did God let Peter look foolish in front of other people when he started acting on words from God? What would you do if God did this to you? Why?

2. Read Exodus 5. What do you think Moses is feeling at each step in this story? What do you learn about God from this episode?

3. To prepare for a ministry open to words from the Lord, Peter fasted while praying and reading the Bible. What is the purpose of fasting in a case like this? What place do you think fasting (on your own or with others) should have in your pursuit of God?

4. What do you make of the physical sensations (warmth, tingling, shaking, falling) that people sometimes have when they experience the Holy Spirit's power? What do you think our attitude should be toward such sensations?

5. Peter's experience of hearing God often seems no more dramatic than ordinary intuition. Would you prefer something more outside your normal experience? Explain.

6. Consider your temperament and the experiences God has used to shape your personality. How do you think the Spirit might speak to you through these?

7. Sometimes God spoke to Peter about someone's physical problem mostly to overcome the person's cynicism, unbelief, or doubt that God cares for them personally. Talk about your own cynicism or that of people you know. Do you think words would affect you or them? Explain.

Chapter 3: The Adventure of Prayer

1. How would you describe your prayer life currently? (Vibrant, lifeless, mostly a one-way listing of your needs, full of gratitude, etc.)

2. What changes would you like to make in your personal prayer life, if any, as a result of what you've read so far?

3. What opportunities do you have to pray with others? How could you make more space in your life

to pray with others and listen to God with others? With whom might you do this?

4. How do you respond to the idea that Jeremiah 31:31–34 applies to you and to people you know? What are the implications of this passage for your life?

5. What is the reason to ask the Lord for a word that can be proved either right or wrong? What do you think about making this a habit in your prayer life?

6. Do you already receive words from the Lord? If so, do they tend to be words that can be tested in light of what actually happens? In your experience, how are words from God different from your own opinions?

7. What can we learn about discernment from the story of Peter's visit to Angela?

8. Gather a group of six to eight people and try the first session of learning to hear and give words, as described in this chapter. Afterward, debrief the experience together. What was helpful? Would you do anything differently next time? Plan a time to go on to the next session if and when your group is ready.

Chapter 4: Proclaim the King and the Kingdom

1. Consider your own influence at your local church. Are there ways you can help to start meetings, or restructure existing ones, so that God is allowed to "direct the traffic" and lead people where they need to be?

2. The Spirit grabbed Bill's attention through dramatic manifestations, but then didn't repeat the drama. What might have been God's reasons for dealing with Bill in this way?

3. Do you believe that our spiritual gifts are at our disposal, like tools in a toolbox, or at the Holy Spirit's disposal, like power tools that need more than our own dexterity to make them work? Or is it more complex than that?

4. Peter lists knowledge, miracles, healing, wisdom, distinguishing between spirits, prophecy, and faith as characteristics of Jesus' own ministry. Which two from the list in 1 Corinthians 12 are not included here? Why do you think that is?

5. When praying for someone, Peter urges you to say whatever you think the Spirit is prompting you to say, however insignificant it may seem to you personally. What is the purpose of doing this?

6. How do you respond to the idea that God might give you a word for someone who doesn't yet know Him? Is this something you would actively pray for? Explain.

7. If you're meeting with a group, spend some time praying together. Ask the Holy Spirit to come and speak to you. Pray especially for guidance on when, where, how, and with whom to proclaim God's kingdom. Respond to what you believe you hear. (Remember that the Spirit is not obliged to give you words.) Afterward, debrief the experience together. What is going well? Are you experiencing any challenges?

Chapter 5: Healing the Emotions

1. Peter says that when he prays for someone, he does not try to guide what is going on in the person's mind or heart. Is it easy for you to deliberately ignore your own preconceived ideas and let God do what He wants to do?

2. What are the benefits of ministering faithfully without trying to control the outcome? What are the risks? Where do ego and fear fit in?

3. What does this mean: "The key to understanding the incident in Gethsemane is this: *Emotions are*

neutral." What are the implications for your ministry to others?

4. Have you experienced healing of emotions? If so, what were the key steps along the path?

5. What role do the psalms of lament (such as Psalm 88) have in your prayer life? Why? What helpful role might they have?

6. What healing of emotions might God want to do in your faith community? Pray about this.

7. What does it mean to turn and face the pain? How does the story of Thomas and Jesus illuminate this idea? How can a community help a deeply wounded person turn and face the pain in a way that leads to healing? What can your community do in this area?

Chapter 6: Healing the Sick

1. What has been your experience, if any, of seeing God heal people physically?

2. One could pray for everyone in a meeting who wants prayer for healing, or one could ask God for words and focus prayer on the people for whom God gives words. What are the pros and cons of each approach?

3. How does a special word from the Holy Spirit affect the person for whom we are praying? How does it affect those who are praying for the person?

4. Do you think having a designated team pray before a meeting increases the likelihood of receiving words about whom to pray for? Explain your thoughts on this.

5. Talk about authority from God to heal the sick. Who do you believe has it? Under what circumstances? How can you know?

6. Have you ever needed discernment from God as to how to minister to someone? How does discernment like that come to us? What can we do to seek it?

7. What do you think we should do if we hold a meeting to pray for healing and receive no words about whom God wants to heal? Or do you think that if we go to God consistently and in humility, He will speak?

Chapter 7: Setting the Captives Free

1. What has been your experience of the demonic, if any? What is your general response to the stories of the demonic in this chapter?

2. Do you believe Christians as well as non-Christians can be afflicted by demons? Explain.

3. How did words help Peter deal with demons? How can listening to the Holy Spirit for words help us deal effectively with demonic activity?

4. Why is it important to understand that demons appear to thrive on sin? How does knowing this help us deal with them?

5. When the curate was trying to deal with a demon, God didn't give him the word that it was a demon of madness. He gave the word to Peter eventually. What do you learn from this situation?

6. What are the risks of being open to words about demonic activity? How can we minimize these risks while still being open to what the Holy Spirit might want us to do?

7. Do you think you could rely on God to give you a word in a situation with a demon? Explain.

Chapter 8: Signs and Blunders

1. How does it affect you to read about cases when Peter was embarrassingly wrong about a word?

2. How do you respond to Peter's argument that New
    Testament prophets were more fallible than the Old
    Testament prophets? Look up some of the biblical
    passages he cites, and assess whether you think he's
    right.

3. Because we can make mistakes in receiving and giv-
    ing words, chapter nine will address testing words.
    But from what you've read so far, what are some
    of the ways you would weigh and test words you
    receive? How would you weigh words others in
    your community receive?

4. What are the implications of being God's *adult*
    children?

5. Why is this statement important? "Our aim is not
    to know more, to hear more words, or to become
    more certain in our faith—it is to *know Him.*"

Chapter 9: Test Everything

1. Why is it essential to test what we believe we hear
    from God? Why test words from others?

2. In practice, how would you go about testing whether
    a word (one you receive directly or from someone
    else) contradicts or is supported by Scripture?

3. How would you put the test of trial and error into practice in your faith community?

4. What are some examples of damage that might be done if a word is wrong? What are examples of good that might be done if it is right?

5. Give an example of a hypothetical word that would be a change of direction for you. What might be a word that follows a well-worn path for you—the kind of thing you might think of on your own?

6. How does having a group of leaders pray together for words and other matters before a meeting begins aid the testing of words?

7. It's great to pass on a word about God's mercy, but what if you feel He has burdened you with a warning or even a word of judgment?

8. What might be a good protocol for your community to test words that are to be given either publicly or privately to another person?

Chapter 10: Facing the End

1. What do you make of the fact that someone who had done healing prayer for years died of an illness

at a relatively young age? What can we learn from
this?

2. Where do you see God at work in the final chapter
    of Peter's life?

3. What are the main insights you will take away from
    reading this book? What practical steps will you
    take in light of these insights?

NOTES

Chapter 1: The God Who Speaks

1. Stuart Y. Blanch, *The World Our Orphanage* (London: The Epworth Press, 1972), 7.

Chapter 3: The Adventure of Prayer

1. George Bernard Shaw, "Saint Joan," in *Our Dramatic Heritage*, ed. Philip G. Hill, vol. 5, *Reactions to Realism* (Cranbury, NJ: Associated University Press, 1991), 112.

2. John Wesley, *The Journal of the Rev. John Wesley* (London: J. Kershaw, 1827), 1:97.

Chapter 5: Healing the Emotions

1. Henry Francis Lyte, "Praise, my soul, the King of heaven" (1834). www.oremus.org/hymnal/p/p058.html.

Chapter 6: Healing the Sick

1. John V. Taylor, *The Go-Between God* (London: SCM Press Ltd, 1972), 212.

Chapter 8: Signs and Blunders

1. Wayne Grudem, *The Gift of Prophecy* (Wheaton, IL: Crossway, 2000), 21–24.

2. Ibid., 27.

3. John R. W. Stott, *The Message of Acts* (Leicester, England: InterVarsity Press, 1994), 324.